Promises to Keep

'Words are for those with promises
to keep.'

W. H. Auden, 'Their Lonely Betters'

Promises to Keep

Thoughts in old age

R<small>ICHARD</small> H<small>OGGART</small>

continuum

Continuum
The Tower Building
11 York Road
London SE1 7NX

15 East 26th Street
New York
NY 10010

www.continuumbooks.com

First published 2005

British Library Cataloguing-in-Publication Data
A catalogue record for this book is available from the British Library.

ISBN: 0–8264–8714–9

While every effort has been made to obtain permissions from owners
of copyright material produced herein, the publishers would like to
apologize for any omissions and will be pleased to incorporate any
missing acknowledgements in the future.

Typeset by Free Range Book Design & Production
Printed and bound in Great Britain by Cromwell Press, Trowbridge, Wiltshire

Contents

Contents

Contents

Introduction – Origins

This book began as a bundle of unordered notes, about the realization that old age had come upon me, surprisingly. Belated, that was: in my eighties.

From thinking about what old age brought with it there arose also thoughts about the approach to death; which may by now not be far off.

Gradually but more and more I also began to look back, and through that inverted telescope tried to reconsider the main elements of our lives. Not the 'and then and then's of a straight narrative. That would more properly belong to an autobiography, and I wrote one of those years ago. Rather: the public events and ideas which have throughout interested me, and their intertwinings with personal life. Such as the family; above all: politics and the family; the intellectual life; belief and morals; words and writing; the power of memory. All of these as looked at again through that time-telescope.

This is not a theoretic or abstract record. Its argument is throughout, or as far as possible, illustrated by incidents and anecdotes from our/my own life. 'This and that happening', it is implying, helped for good or ill to direct thought in this or that way.

It then seemed sensible to bracket that long look back within the two main areas of thought which had set them off. So: the first realization of growing old became Chapter 1; and then, after seven chapters on the issues and ideas which have most concerned us/me over that near-century, came finally the thoughts on the approach to Death. Sober but resilient – and cheerful at times – are those pages; I like to think.

It would be excessive even to call all this an 'intellectual autobiography'. 'A look back over main concerns, within the perspective offered by great age and the sense of the nearness of death', is wordy, but would be more accurate.

Every life is in some senses unique; all lives share some elements. It would be mistaken, at least for one with my cast of mind, to try to describe the shared elements – the common human experiences – without aiming to give them the particular colour and flavour of particular lives. So I have tried to do that; in the hope that some experience will be shared; and that enough, though particular and even peculiar, will have its own kind of interest.

RICHARD HOGGART

Though nothing can bring back the hour
Of splendour in the grass, of glory in the flower;
We will grieve not, rather find
Strength in what remains behind.

(William Wordsworth, 'Ode: Intimations of
Immortality from Recollections
of Early Childhood')

Chapter 1

Realizing that Old Age Has Arrived

I am a very foolish, fond old man.

(Shakespeare, *King Lear*)

Prologue

I go for a short, late afternoon walk along pavements crowded with school-children of various ages heading for home, most of them continuously laughing, joshing – a good word, that last. I do not envy them. It was lovely to be young; only a curmudgeon would begrudge them that part of life. A slight regret and one kept well in check is all I register. I can remember that time, and warmly, indeed happily; and try dispassionately to imagine how they see me now, a slow old man with a stick.

Some make way for me politely. Others look at me as at one from another planet, to which they cannot conceive themselves ever arriving. A very few look at me as though I am a bit of a nuisance, slowing things down. Hardly any will see me as a survivor because that would link them emotionally with one who was once their age but now occupies a point in space and time towards which they do not yet see themselves slowly moving, an outcome they cannot easily conceive. Hazlitt in this as in so many

1

aphorisms caught the dominant mood: 'No young man feels he shall ever die' ('The feeling of Immortality in Youth').

Those who can in spirit move out from their peers and sympathize with old people are rare and wonderful types. Another one, I remember from many years ago, remarked, at about 17, that he could not accept the thought of being 30; clearly, that would be unbearably joyless. Many, perhaps most before 20, assume that all passion will be spent when they do arrive at that third decade. Then there comes to mind George Moore, celebrating the sexual attractions of women 'of a certain age' – 30.

—

In the following pages I will switch between 'I', 'one', 'you', 'us', 'we' as seems best, though 'I' is likely to be predominant. With all their obvious and inevitable limitations, these are observations on, chiefly, one man's experience of growing up, of becoming old, and of beginning to face the idea of death. Hence so many 'I's. But it is assumed that many others are sharing such kinds of experience, especially of family, relationships, occupations, space, time and much else; and particularly if they have reached, say, 55 and above. Hence the other pronouns used here. In another sense none of us will share many experiences, since lives in the one country or area or occupation can vary widely. So it would be misleading to generalize too much; better, then, to use where necessary the personal pronoun and example, and trust that those too may as often as possible have some wider interest and perhaps implications.

I have used a lot of inverted commas. These are usually to indicate where I am drawing upon common speech; which, given the theme, is full and rich.

First Indications

Bacon, as so often, put the case with supreme simplicity: 'Age creeps upon us unawares.' Tolstoy spoke for many when he noted in his Diary that: 'Old age is the most unexpected of all things that can happen to a man.'

It steals up like a burglar in stockinged feet, but with a cosh; *that* we at last feel, and cannot evade. Since old age has no universal, fixed, starting date, the popular proverb is right too; well, a rough guide: 'You are only as old as you feel.' Some people decide to be old at 65, when they 'retire', which rightly sounds like walking backwards, out of sight; begin to draw the State Old Age Pension and settle for pipe-and-slippers. Some of us take the pension but ignore the indicated age and suddenly realize, perhaps at 80, that we have become old – as my wife and I did. Even that need not mean that a shutter has come down; at 80-plus you can go on expecting to write the next book or doing whatever engrosses you. You can still 'look forward', in your head be intermittently an adolescent, if you will and are lucky; chiefly with your health. A light covering of snow or a warm June evening can please you as they always have, and needn't always bring thoughts of mortality. Nor does, if you can manage it, a morning of non-routine shopping. You have to learn to be old, but in the right, not the decrepit, ways.

Phases

You may then look back and begin dividing life into phases, such as: one to twenty – growing up; twenty to sixty-odd – family and career; sixty-odd to who knows when? – but that is the first totally free phase; to do what you want.

3

Looked at in another way, those phases can each seem both short and long, expandable or contractible, chiefly according to their emotional weights in the memory. Those twenty years since retirement can seem a short phase when set against the six-and-a-bit of the decades before, roughly a third of those filled with growing up; and then forty-odd years of the differing, often demanding, but almost always enjoyable, activities of family and profession. Viewed in that perspective, this last score of years, busy though they too have proved to be, can seem little more than a fag end. Yet a baby born just when I retired could now be married and a parent. It is, though this is hard to absorb mentally, an unusually lengthy fag end. But not at all, even at 87, as wearisome as the fiftieth Psalm describes existence at 80: 'Though men be so strong that they come to fourscore years [no doubt very long in the days of the Psalmist] yet is their strength then but labour and sorrow.' Not altogether, nowadays.

'Blocks' or 'clusters' are better labels than 'phases'. Their differing weights in the memory, according to events and busy-ness, could be indicated by numbers: from birth to the end of adolescence would have 10 points, your twenties to forties would be 15, the fifth and sixth decades 20 and the period of retirement 5. But that is too worldly and mechanical. One needs a more intricately shaded approach, one which recognizes that periods overlap, are semi-concurrent, not always in temporal sequence.

I will not attempt that now. What is clearer and simpler is the fact that it is possible, without undervaluing the warmth of any one period, to discover which of them is still most dear to us. That proves to have been when the children were, roughly, 14, 12 and 8; that would be about 1960. All were still at home and not fully spreading their wings, enjoying the pursuits of their generation outside the home, but not constantly looking outside for all interests and amusements, still feeling that part of their whole being belonged within that circle of five.

Further Indications

Let us, however, take 80 as the first unmistakeable gateway to old age for more and more people these days. You are from now living on what is casually called 'borrowed time'; whatever that may mean. You can't borrow from Chance or Fate or Physical Condition. 'Unexpected time' would be less picturesque but more exact. You have arrived at a place which displays the first sign for the last bus, and are in the queue, with the survivors. You recall then Emily Dickinson's finely laconic, unenthusiastic reception of Death's carriage, which kindly stopped for her because she was disinclined to hail it.

And I recall a relative who at 70-something was courted by one she did not accept, but kindly described as 'a very clean old man'. That consideration is by then important. A philosophical friend also in his eighties rather sadly mused that he was 'too often aware of my crotch these days'. That recalls a comic memory, from 1946. On the way to being demobilized, a couple of us, a journalist and I, spent a week crossing a hot Europe from south to north by slow train, and were soon much aware of our crotches. We passed some time inventing copy for 'Critch', a sovereign cure.

Nowadays other, external, indications of age begin to appear; you feel then like remaindered or discarded stock, on the shelf until its time for pulping comes. A few years ago I was asked to give a rather prestigious Annual Lecture. Encouraging. Later I learned that the organizers had been suddenly let down by the speaker they had engaged, and had decided to try me – but only after they had asked a good acquaintance whether I was by now 'past it'.

Arguing that museologists should connect their discipline more with the world outside, the occasion went well; though none of the professionals present came up to me afterwards. The museum, as promised, issued my lecture. As compared with its single predecessor, which was properly printed and bound, mine appeared simply on typed and clipped A4 paper. For inventing status symbols the English would be hard to beat; the professionals had not greatly liked the message.

I could 'bridle' (lovely word) at the assumption that you can have little to say at 80-odd. After all, Sophocles wrote three tragedies in his early eighties; *Electra* has a particular modern relevance, in its analysis of a society given to shameless expediency. Titian painted magnificent pictures at 88. Verdi was composing into his eighties. Adenauer was the first Chancellor of the Federal Republic of Germany from the ages of 73 to 87 and died at 91. Irving Berlin died at 101. Alistair Cooke was still broadcasting weekly at 95 and died only a few weeks after what proved to be his last 'Letter for the BBC'. John Gielgud was still working in television a month before he died, at 96. That lot should cheer up any octogenarian.

For your part you decide, among other modest resolutions, not to make use of any of those wise old owl phrases such as: 'I don't know what the world is coming to these days'; 'You can't put an old head on young shoulders'; and 'As t'old cock crows, so t'young 'un learns.' You try to take care not to become what crude people behind their hands might be tempted to call 'a boring old fart', whose endless anecdotes of the past are increasingly hard to bear. 'Anecdotage', a friend calls that; though Disraeli coined it first.

Very often, you recall how glad you are that you had children; not only for late help and comfort, though those are invaluable, but for the sustenance of the intangible bonds of mutual affection with them and with their children. What sort of person would you have grown into if you had had neither wife nor children? Self-engrossed, lonely, odd is my first guess.

Your loving and thoughtful daughter and son-in-law suggest you should now move near them, so that they can 'keep an eye on you'. You agree gratefully, and discover that there is nothing which so taxes and fully confirms your age as a late house-move. The physical but, more important, the mental shake-up can truly be called traumatic. After 26 years of your presence the old house seems to groan as you disembody it. It didn't expect this, and nor did the two of you. You realize for the first time that a house long lived in becomes as if a part of your own personalities, not easily to be shucked off.

You are extremely lucky to be going near, but not with, the closest of relatives. You love one another across the generations, but eventually there would have been emotional strains were you all in the same house. They have found a manageable house for you about three hundred yards from them. Fine.

What would you have done otherwise? Then you recall Montaigne and his choice of a quiet place behind the shop. What would be the modern equivalent? A place detached and preferably in a quiet enclave near a medium-sized city centre, with a large sitting/dining room, two bedrooms or three, and full 'facilities'; lots of room for books, a phone, a telly, a hi-fi, a PC, a printer – what a lot of baggage can seem the comfortable minimum nowadays – and an Alarm Button. Meals and company nearby, if wanted. No rules other than those which safety regulations and concern for others require. Very cushioned, compared with Montaigne.

We are very lucky; the house they have found for us meets virtually all those specifications; and of course some even more familial, handy. As Norbert Elias pointed out, even the best retirement home can lack an essential quality, 'homeliness'. The smell can make the difference.

A last modern addition to the above list needs to be made: that when the time comes for you each to be carried out horizontally it will be done without fuss, in a cardboard coffin, and taken to one of those woodland burial places. There is one just outside Norwich, that environmentally conscious city. It would of course be very much better if Fate allowed you to go together.

The pattern of the year can now be at first glance almost blank, no foreign trips pencilled in, few visits in or out, to you or by you. Almost all weeks adhere to a new almost fixed pattern, each day with its pale colouring: Tuesday and Friday, shopping; Thursday, outside help on the house and garden; Monday and Wednesday blank and so perhaps offering each week just a hint of something new and interesting. The weekend still feels rather special, as it did when you were fully at work, and as it no doubt still does to believers; nowadays it rarely honours that preliminary feeling.

The above is probably the minimum set pattern and so not quite adequate. It has to be filled in, pleasantly filled in if we are lucky: with long-neglected reading or rereading; crosswords; and, best of all, writing – trying to make sense of what it has all been about. By then the pattern can be quite well coloured.

The daily newspapers can begin to seem increasingly concerned about matters which, from your new perspective, are not worth all that time and attention. They seem, broadsheets and populist, more trivial than they were twenty or thirty years ago. No doubt that is due to the competition, and perhaps even more to the threat from the Internet.

Some people try to comfort you by remarking that the eighties are 'a good age' to have reached, or 'a ripe old age' or even 'The Golden Years'. What strange epithets those can be. They cannot mean 'well lived' or 'virtuous', though they might seem to carry a small degree of congratulation, the assumption that to live so long you must have 'taken good care of yourself', which sounds selfish. To you it doesn't seem that any kinds of compliment are called for. They belong to the order of things which Henry James called 'cheap comforts'. Such favoured idioms, nowadays often invented by the Public Relations industry, are forms of escape, together with: 'Senior Citizens', 'The Years of Seniority', 'The Mature Years', 'The Autumn Years'. Obviously, all try to avoid 'The Declining Years', 'The Second Childhood' and, of course, any reference to 'Senility' or 'Senescence'.

Hardly ever used words tend now and again to creep into the mind. 'Sombre', for instance; a fine, small word whose low rumbling echoes its meaning well. Perhaps it indicates occasional low feelings, such as that it is not attractive to think that you might reach 90. On another day that doesn't seem too bad a fate, as some people you have met have apparently found. So the would-be-will, ever on the saving alert, starts cautiously offering 95 as a just possible future. But – perhaps not.

Meanwhile – odd, this, but only one of several modest indicative assumptions – at 80-odd you are, in restaurants, no longer the one to whom the waiter hands the bill as to the presumed Head of the Family. No point in waving for it. The old man is obviously being taken out for a treat. The bill is given, with a slight conspiratorial flick of the eye, to one who is a generation back. You restore your pride, if it really needs restoring, by insisting on paying the bill. A strange little dance.

Coping with the Body

The body had better be looked at early because it is increasingly, if not preoccupying, rather importunate. More often than you have been used to, it reminds you that parts – legs, odd other muscles, hearing, sight – are beginning to need special attention; probably 'wearing out' would be a more accurate term. Muscular energy appears to have lost some of its powers of renewal. It is a very long time since a colleague in America called out: 'You look bright-eye'd and bushy-tailed today.' Pills and potions begin to appear at the bedside. Getting out of bed becomes a slightly achy daily reminder that things are not quite as they used to be; my wife still manages it at 6.30.

You have to pee fairly often, but don't yet seem due for a prostate operation; and can hold your water for a surprisingly long time, if on a platform or long car journey. Mind controls matter then, but you may have to run for it when released.

You read a few relevant articles and practise a few geriatric exercises. 'Going for a good walk' is more easily said than done. That slight stroll has been substituted. Sometimes you feel mildly miffed that, even at 80-odd, such obstructions have appeared. You remember Lance, the former LSE Reader who danced on his daughter's table on New Year's Eve, just before his hundredth birthday. Mind you, he died about six weeks later. Heroic.

So by now you have help with the eyes and ears, which are not much of a problem; the teeth, minus two or three, are not in bad shape. The three other senses do not greatly occupy you, and do not seem the sort of thing which calls for a visit to the doctor. Taste and touch are apparently in good order; and most of all smell, the most earthy sense, keeps its often privileged place. As it did for George Orwell, who used it as a moral probe; he could *smell* derelictions of many kinds. My own is just a creaturely nose but reacts well, from lavender to farts; it still serves.

Logically, the sex drive fits between body and mind, but may as well appear here and now. It seems to have wound down and, though one remembers its expression not like Sophocles – 'a mad and savage master' – but with great pleasure, one does not yearn for it or think of trying Viagra. That would be daft at our age. And a solid foundation of lived-in-love has moved to the front. But it is still amusing to recall James Agate's story of Clemenceau on his eightieth birthday, catching sight of a pretty girl and exclaiming: 'Oh, to be seventy again!' Very French, direct and unabashed. The Champs Elysées was the perfect setting for such an encounter: the Old Politician and the Pretty Girl.

So, though the ability to take that 'good long walk' is impaired, you may still hope, with NHS help, eventually to regain the power for a quiet and steady stroll through the nearby North Norfolk countryside. Then, to adapt Belloc on the great hills of the South Country, the great hills of the North Country come back into my mind. Oh, to go again to the love of your youth, the Yorkshire Dales; just once more – Wharfedale, Nidderdale, Wensleydale, Swaledale; and all the dependent dales and the rivers and slopes sheltering them. Perhaps it may be possible one day to go up there again, in someone else's car.

Does one wish to be young or at least younger again? Not really; too much hassle. Jonathan Swift caught the right dismissive note: 'No wise man ever wished to be younger.' Yet more and more we may realize, and not only because we are ourselves in that final phase, that we should when young cherish the old. Or at least let them depart in peace. They have almost certainly had their troubles, and may still have; of the body and mind. One remembers then Yeats, in 'The Circus Animals' Desertion', feeling when old that he had a tin-can tied to his tail, a dragging, not to be removed, thing. And Herbert's 'Grace', on Death always 'working like a mole' on us.

If some thoughtlessly push you aside in a queue, others redress the balance – by offering you their seat on a train or tube. There are still more of those than of the pushers.

Somewhere near here a few minor embarrassments are recalled; as when you splash out and propose to buy some new item of clothing, perhaps items which might be expected to 'see you out': a suit or hat. And you are told that they are 'not right', because they are 'not your age', make you look younger than you are, which is not felt to be desirable. Is anyone ever warned off an item of clothing because 'it makes you look too old?' Clothing for your time of life is not easily found. There are specialist shops for fat men and women; under a suitable pseudonym. One does not or only very rarely find one which explicitly caters for the old. Perhaps more exist, disguised as catering 'For those of Mature Years'. Incidentally, at that point as so often you can be glad if your work has not required you daily to cripple the English language, as do so many jobs today. But, anyway, buy what you want; it can be a bargain for someone at Oxfam later, with all the hacking jackets and gabardine trousers; you could precisely locate a subculture from an afternoon in Oxfam. Meanwhile, plead that: 'it will see me out' for items you really love and will keep.

Relatively small matters annoy more because they seem to be indicators of a growing loss of everyday intuitive control, physical and mental; becoming more clumsy, slightly bumping into chairs and table corners, ineptitude at fitting small objects such as torch batteries into their right spaces, miscalculating the likely weight of things such as dishes and so dropping them, making mistakes with figures at the moment of writing them down, remembering telephone numbers for no more than a couple of minutes – a sort of widespread gradual slippage.

Memory increasingly does not hold, especially of the names which go with faces. Whilst shaving you may think of a few items which must be remembered that day. As you swill your face, they have gone. Oddly, for me a little Pelmanism, picked up from a scoutmaster many years ago, 'connecting by association', still sometimes works. Inevitably, Memory will weave through almost all these pages and will be likely to need fuller attention later on.

The later Yeats appears again, this time forgetting the tin can and insisting, in 'Sailing to Byzantium', that we should be cheerful and let: 'Soul clap its hands and sing, and louder sing / For every tatter in its mortal dress.' Like most of us, Yeats sometimes swung between melancholy and a resilient joy. His moments of joy tend to create the stronger impression. Good.

Coping with the Mind

Here and now, the mind feels fairly supple. But mental changes are more subtle than aches in the limbs and the like; and more destructive. Of that, the shadow of Parkinson's disease and Alzheimer's is never far from reminding us.

Yet the mind, through memory, also offers moments of light-heartedness and warmth, unexpected reminders of life's happier moments. About children, for instance. Our three children have produced many such memories, but for each there is one which demands pride of place: a baby's uninhibited welcoming smiles and bouncings in the pram on the front lawn as, back from work, you come in sight at the gate; a ten-year-old's breakaway rush through the gate and down the platform to meet you at Hull's Paragon Station; the excited panting of a three-year-old about to be given a shoulder ride. And of course many from marriage itself, but most of all our first meeting in a London hotel room after my three years abroad with the army and with still another to go back to, in Italy. It was the summer of 1945 and I had been sent 'home' for a few days to attend an army course on possible problems of 'resettlement'. I was to pass the information to the rest of the regiment. When I was demobilized in the early summer of 1946 my wife had a baby asleep upstairs.

That recalls a slight unrecoverable loss for those of us who met that pattern. In the first few years of marriage, before children appear, there can be an extended honeymoon, a freedom to sleep longer, to travel casually, to go out and stay up late with friends. We missed that since, as I said above, my demobilization almost coincided with the birth of our first child. Of course, the period immediately after the last child leaves home can offer a similar pleasant freedom; similar but not the same. After all, you are thirty or so years older.

In old age, the sense of non-recoverable loss is partnered by that of non-repeatable pleasures: of long walks and longer drives; of all those places you have been lucky enough to visit but are not likely to see again; of loving grandparents, both now dead; of that period when the family was all together and 'looking forward' to various enjoyments. The sense of a continuously unrolling canvas, but one which we can actually roll back for another look, is no longer always present. So many events and things belong to the irrecoverable and irrevocable past. 'Looking forward' survives but is less habitual these days;

'looking backward', through memory, is more frequent; better than nothing, but not a full substitute. Time no longer seems a friend, on your side with pleasures to come. But we can now, if we will, recognize its recuperative value. Jorge Luis Borges added to and developed that: 'Time is the substance I am made of. Time is a river that carries me away. But I am the river.' In youth the future is immensely long, almost inexhaustible. Gradually, age sidles upon us until, unless we are lucky, we sometimes feel drained. In response, we develop a reluctance to change, an urge to shrug off some possible changes or commitments which earlier we would have met as happily acceptable challenges.

It is not that the spirit is willing but the flesh weak; rather, that the spirit has begun to make common cause with the flesh, in being reluctant. A phrase such as: 'Oh, that's too much trouble', which you used rarely, and suspected in those who did habitually use it, you find yourself uttering, or silently recalling, quite often. A counterpart is the less frequent use of: 'I'm really looking forward to …'; its negative form is more often used.

—

Of these, as I have hinted, one of the greatest, perhaps the greatest after death in a family, is changing houses after you reach about 75. This is especially true if you are leaving a comfortably sized house within which you have moved easily for many years whilst amassing stuff around you, as if you are both feeding and being entwined by a group of plants as greedy as the old favourite among working and lower-middle-class people; aspidistras.

Twenty-six and a half years in one place have led imperceptibly to the hope that it will 'see us out'; the phrase we saw as also adopted about favourite clothes. That we are going in response to a deeply concerned offer from a daughter and her husband is naturally an enormous compensation.

Yet the process proves to be like the pulling up of roots many of which you had not been aware of, but which seem to shriek as they succumb and are bundled onto the wagon. They arouse memories like embedded perfumes, or simple but strong smells which transfer to your hands and then to your heart. They begin with the odd minor problems you have grown used to and used to doing nothing about: the stubborn stain on the kitchen floor, the awkward garage up-and-over door, the small steps to the garden which you know 'need attention'. Last-minute treatment can be given to a few of these and similar things. But WD 40, that multi-purpose DIY aid, can't do everything.

The movables must go, either with you or to similar places, thrown or given away: the living-room knick-knacks, duplicate and triplicate kitchen gadgets, a bedspread rendered unneeded by the arrival of duvets, this and that disposition of cushions, pictures and books, the wobbly wooden thing holding flowers on the half-landing; the equally wobbly pair of bedside tables you picked up years ago in a Madrid market.

Nowadays, you discover at this point, many things, including some which are to you agreeable pieces of furniture, can no longer be given away: IKEA is often preferred. The bathroom has a bidet you proudly installed a quarter of a century ago; at that time perhaps one of the few in Farnham. That does not escape criticism from possible buyers because of its colour, as does the bath; no one lives with avocado today. Many of your things, they say kindly, are 'too old-fashioned for our generation'. You are slightly insulted, miffed, abashed on behalf of those things, and feel more out of date yourself. Those who buy homes as 'Job Lots for Clearance' must have an easy and profitable time. Those who bought our house were very agreeable and easy to do business with. But they soon repainted our pale white sittingroom: a shade of red. As I write, someone reports that an estate agent in Muswell Hill (of course) has advised a prospective seller to repaint their sittingroom: from brick red to off-white. 'That would add a thousand to the price.'

When, rather later, I first heard: 'Of course, our generation believe...', I immediately suspected that limited labelling. In some people generational claims join hands with ageism.

Of course, you miss the neighbours you had grown old with. From them you had learned, among other things, that retired regular army officers can be better read and better informed than you and your kind had given them credit for. The academic world has its own kind of limiting assumptions.

The nearness to one's daughter and son-in-law more than makes up for the loss of such connections; but still you miss: the butcher who asks if you have heard the new recording of Strauss's *Four Last Songs*; the plumber whose charges are fair and whose son is a university lecturer; the long view from the bedroom window to the Castle, the Wey valley and the Hog's Back. Coming home by car, nine miles west of Guildford, you drop off the Hog's Back and slide into that shallow valley and see Farnham straddling it comfortably. It is fitting that the oak timbers for the roof of Westminster Hall came from here and that William Cobbett is buried in the churchyard. Farnham looks like and was a friendly place to come home to, especially comely in the early evening light. The equivalent of those losses will no doubt be recovered over time, but time is an increasingly sparse and unreliable element.

However did we manage to leave so apparently effort-lessly, after only one year, the rented half-house in unpre-possessing Redcar? That was getting on for sixty years ago and the answer is simple. The man who moved us to a nearby village told friends that we had 'nowt but bloody coal and bloody books'. Very sensible in those post-war years: to keep warm and have plenty to read. Farnham was the seventh move after Redcar (with Leicester the most warm and manageable for a growing family); and in Farnham the real build-up of *things* reached its climax.

The nearness of close relatives after the last move saves you from the worst shocks of both agoraphobia and claustrophobia. The first because you are now launching yourselves into little-known horizontal space which at first you neither know nor control. Claustrophobia threatens because at the start your habitual daily space, your known world, has been enclosed. In short, and the simple phrasing does define the new world, you lack some *customary ways* and things, outward and inward. So you set about establishing markers in the area, from doctor to newsagent and so on and on. And eventually you take it all for granted; you have adapted.

You know that wherever you go there will be all around you a retirement culture: Golf, Bowls, the Public Library, Church and Chapel, all kinds of special interest groups. Fine, for many people, though heavily favouring men's pursuits. We are neither clubby nor hobbyish. We, along with some others, female and male, will remain satisfied with books and other private pursuits. Luckily, good books old and new, and from several sources, stand instantly and always available; and *The Oldie* is cheering; TV and, even more, radio, still provide some good programmes. To some degree: 'the world forgetting by the world forgot' sounds sufficient, not meagre.

Junk mail – especially for hearing aids, all kinds of vitamin pills, more charities than you knew existed and those more inventive in their pleas than you had realized. Obviously, you are on a vast and class-graded mailing list, massively exchanged.

Ever since you first 'retired' there have been only a few public occasions for both of you to dress up. For you, in a good suit, well-ironed shirt and careful tie. The two of you scarcely think of such things. But you need to take care that casualness doesn't become carelessness and then perhaps unnoticed 'shabbiness'. That last was a word of great weight in our childhoods, often applied to people who had – sadly – 'let themselves go'. 'We can't have you going out, all shabby like that.' Waiters in mufti often look like that, as they head for home; one always feels rather sorry for them.

Behind all the above transformations is that now firm knowledge that, in the second half of your eighties, you have become survivors, who did not expect to last so long.

That as if final sense occurred strongly when I paid a visit to the very centre of Leeds, after a long gap. I stood and looked. The nineteenth-century Town Hall, which once had looked huge and grand, now seemed more of an assertion to the grandiose, one in the eye for Bradford. In the thirties the 'City Fathers', short of space, added the Civic Hall, a few hundred yards away. We schoolchildren were conscripted to stand in line and cheer as someone important passed, to declare the Hall open.

After Munich, Milan, Florence, Barcelona, Madrid, Strasbourg, Seville, Bordeaux, Leeds suggests that the English sense of 'The City' as a coherent, liveable-within entity has hardly existed. Put that down to our early Industrial Revolution and the urban squalor of huge industries, and rank after rank of mean streets to house the workers, among which I grew up. To that was added the assertion of big city self-consciousness through these large public buildings.

They say Leeds is renewing itself successfully. I wonder. Or is it now becoming a globalized, brand-obsessed, meritocrats' shopping and business centre, something which could be plonked down almost anywhere, with no longer any Yorkshire roots? Still, the Dales are safe: so far.

Now for the long look back.

Chapter 2

Great and Terrible Happenings

It takes a great deal of history to produce a little literature.

(Henry James, *Life of Nathaniel Hawthorne*)

The Issues

Henry James may well be right. The almost complete century through which people of our age have lived has certainly seen a great deal of history, if that is taken to mean events of enormous, even terrifying, importance. It has also produced at least 'a little literature'; and perhaps more than that.

Obviously, other centuries and continents have had their horrors. Our horrors stand out for their combination of geographical spread, physical scale, administrative and technological complexity and ideological justifications. They challenge the belief in progress by whoever that is held and whether they are religious believers or not.

—

It may be useful briefly to recall at this early point some of the most important of those events and some of the ways

21

in which they were discussed and presented to us, chiefly by writers (and, of course, broadcasters) of various kinds.

This century saw, then, two World Wars and a number of others not quite so extensive, such as that over Korea. Between the big wars came a worldwide depression which, among much else, in some places fuelled outward-looking aggression. In 1938 Chamberlain had come back from his visit to Hitler waving his piece of paper: 'This means peace in our time.' That day I was calling on one of my aunts, who was greatly relieved. I told her I thought Chamberlain had been tricked. That brought sharp words about the 'clever clogs' at university.

Then the war ended, and after that 'real' life seemed to begin; in about mid-1946. I got my first job, as a literature tutor in university extramural education.

But quite soon the 'Iron Curtain' divided Europe as did its partner the Cold War, which lasted more than four decades. Later, the Berlin Blockade and Berlin Wall, and Vietnam. Who can forget that photograph of a little Vietnamese girl, naked and burned with napalm, fleeing screaming down a road? Or that of the cold-blooded murder, in the street with a bullet to the head, of a North Vietnamese captive by a South Vietnamese Brigadier of Police. That murderer passed his last decades running a restaurant in the USA. It can be guessed that he had many curious customers there. As the last decade of the century began, the Soviet Empire collapsed. This list has the minimum of entries; to go further would be to treble or quadruple its length.

—

Two other institutions need to be given a special place because of their appalling nature. I say 'institutions' to underline that both lasted for years. One is the Soviet

Gulag, which began in 1918 under Lenin and reached its peak under Stalin; the other is the Nazi Holocaust, which was in the making in the late thirties and put into full effect during the Second World War. I imagine that there will be no dissent from the assertion that, in Europe, no other events of the century equalled those two for inhumanity. It is difficult to overstress their importance and effects.

They had, of course, strikingly different origins. The originators of the Holocaust, the Nazis, apart from some inevitable elements of resistance, carried the bulk of their largely educated people with them. Among much else, they were anxious to shake off the memory of 1918's defeat. As so often, Tocqueville has a sentence on this: 'To commit violent or unjust acts, it is not necessary for a government to have ['in the beginning' – my insert] the will or even the power; the habits, ideas and passions of the time must lend themselves to their committal.' Tocqueville adds: 'It is far easier to act under conditions of tyranny than to think.'

In this particular perspective, the emergence of Soviet Communism is less socially complex than the rise of Nazism. Its continuous protestations of national concurrence, its smothering propaganda, were, especially under Stalin, imposed on a people, most of whom were illiterate serfs; but who had been for centuries, through Church and Tsar, taught to worship Mother Russia.

The attempt to assess comparative awfulness is difficult. Nazism was ideologically driven and above all technologically carried out. Soviet Communism's cruelties were less ideologically driven in that they did not emerge logically from the Communist Revolution, but from the minds of some of those who had led the Revolution: at their worst, in full force, they were driven by one man, Stalin. The Gulag effected the brutal imprisonment or extermination of millions in pursuit of the totally managed, the entirely subservient, society. Compared with Nazism, it was in its methods only slightly technological, preferring to work its millions of prisoners to death or, for sufficiently important convicted 'criminals', to use suitably old-fashioned methods, such as the single bullet through the back of the head. Behind it all was also the drive to industrialize Russia.

The Holocaust was, in the cant but handy modern phrase, 'something else'. It was driven without pity or remorse by a brutal philosophy; Soviet Communism had the initial excuse that it was driven by the aim of improving its society. Nazism asserted that some people, notably Jews and Gypsies, were not worth living space; and then used modern technology to follow, actually to realize, the implications of that conviction. The supreme image of this horror was to be found in the concentration camps; and here joined hands, in part, with Stalin.

With such things one tends to discover that a single image, which may not be the bloodiest or most evident, sticks in the mind and stands for the whole. Mine came in an anecdote from one survivor. He recalled that at night in his lower bunk he had grown used to the pee of the man above leaking onto him. Relatively small as it is, that image suggests something of the constant, the lived-through, dehumanization.

Those two operations, one continuing well after the war, began to be generally better recognized and assessed in Britain only in the 1950s and 1960s. A larger number began slowly to know about them in the following decades. Most got on with their lives, emotional attachments, domestic worries, ambitions; and relegated such revelations to remote and almost closed spaces in the mind. Fully to face them was, from one perspective, essential; but life must go on. From another perspective, amnesia operates.

Here one remembers *Macbeth:* 'These deeds must not be thought / After these ways; so, it will make us mad'; or from the same play the more taut: 'Things without all remedy / Should be without regard.'

Responses

My wife and I were born towards the end of the First World War and so have been aware of political and other events since the early thirties. To recall Henry James quoted above: what 'literature' – in a broad sense – nourished us?

Among many others, I again select some of the most telling: Orwell's *Animal Farm* and *1984*, Yeats, T. S. Eliot, Auden, Sartre, Camus, Edmund Wilson, Hemingway, a little of Freud, Niebuhr, Arendt, Arnold Toynbee, Günther Grass, Primo Levi, Kafka, Beckett, Pinter, Larkin – to name only a few as they come to mind, and not in chronological order. Squashed together like that they may evoke something of the swirling intellectual and imaginative flavour of those decades, for two reasonably well-educated citizens.

I say 'citizens' because the focus here will not be on the events themselves but on how individuals and groups in English society responded to them. In looking first at those who have been lucky enough to receive higher education I shall try to avoid large generalizations but will concentrate on our own family life. In its social and political interests it has been to some degree typical – rather like the lives of a fair-sized number of people similarly placed – in its actions and responses, failures and successes.

We were and are *Guardian* readers, Labour Party members and the predictable rest; though some of our friends have become Liberal Democrats. We welcomed the post-war Labour victory, and were very pleased with the Attlee government's early successes, especially the founding of the National Health Service. We were in favour of the voluntary dissolution of Empire, though we came eventually to recognize that there were some ameliorating aspects to all that. We did not learn this at school; there, we learned chiefly about the benefits imperialism had brought to benighted peoples after the initial and unchallenged bravery of the Tommies through which those lands had been conquered. Having had a working-class father who had taken the Queen's shilling and gone to fight the Boers, I was an early mistruster of the Imperial Saga. My wife's father had been wounded in the First World War and thereafter did not utter a word about it.

On a different plane, we learned of the enormous advance in genetics, particularly made by Crick and Watson's discovery in 1953 of the structure of DNA. And we were awed and fascinated by the move into space.

Much later, we were cheered by the collapse of the Soviet Empire; but also saddened. Earlier we had hoped for much there, for a humane communist and communal nation, a successful social dream, experiment and achievement. Even so, we were suspicious of some of the early books whose authors came back from Russia hailing uncritically the achievements of the New Society. Quite soon, we were more Koestlerish and Orwellian than far-Left socialists, let alone Communists.

We had grown up in the thirties and entered married life immediately after the war, when the instruments of mass communication – the press and magazines, radio and then television – had begun with great speed to establish themselves as the massive and repetitive voices of society.

In no other era had people been so constantly talked to. How did we respond to all the voices, especially to those which warned us of the increasing horrors across Europe, and in particular of the Gulag and the Holocaust. At such moments, one wryly recalls Ortega y Gasset's remark that: 'It is not obligatory for a nation to have great men.' One agrees, with relief. Then one remembers Churchill during the last war. Everything can depend on what type of great man.

As to ourselves, we did not march, with or without banners. Was this a dereliction? Possibly. Certainly we were deeply unwilling to do such things, or to hear marchers as they went past chanting: 'What do we want? We want...'. We particularly disliked hearing teachers taking part in such demonstrations and chants. That kind of thing was too near to being mindless, in the end too reminiscent of football crowds. I put this down to our shared undemonstrative and rather puritanical backgrounds; but it was deep-seated and did not mean that we had no firm political views. When in autumn 1956 Eden ordered the Suez intervention we might well have marched, had we not been in America.

In his *Politics*, Aristotle said that man was by nature a political animal. But there are different ways of being political and we were of the inward persuasion. We understood at one level Thomas Mann's statement that every intellectual attitude is latently political ('given this or that political belief, what are you going to do about it?'). But we read that first as a statement about the necessary character of intellectual life, which may also be a call to direct political action by individuals. I at least, perhaps too readily, agreed with Shaw's: 'The man who writes about himself and his own time is the only man who writes about all people and about all time.' That could propose too wide a net and be something of a self-justification.

We concentrated, as did most people, on bringing up the children as well as we could. We followed political events here and abroad quite closely; but more to the front of our minds would come, for example, the fear that one child might have the measles. This can seem natural enough but did push out of full attention, or to the margins of attention, the fate of the prisoners of Siberia or of the Jews who had been herded into concentration camps and eventual death. We were the lucky ones but did not always recognize just how lucky we were. We gave money to relevant good causes, sometimes wrote to our MPs, but engaged in little more direct public action. Was there more we could have done, as individual citizens, short of marching? Yes, we could have done much more, been more active in bearing witness against evils we could not avoid seeing; such as Apartheid; and especially the Gulag, which lasted long into the Cold War.

I can make two relatively small pleas in mitigation here. I did pay a lot of attention to the condition of English life, its disabling sense of class, its inadequate educational system and the errors of the mass media of communication as they developed. I wrote and gave talks whenever invitations came, and broadcast. I hope that had some effect on some people but, looking from now back over the years, I think it was too enclosed, too Little Englandish.

The second excuse is to blame the newly and almost overwhelmingly present mass media. To some degree they did alert us to what was going on over the water. They did not do enough. They hate to rock the boat. It is not in their interest to make their readers, listeners, viewers unhappy. To keep up and expand sales they have to be to a large extent cheer-leaders. They will flatter us that we live in a stable and sane society (which is an exaggeration) and are disinclined to be doom-mongers. So they concentrate on what cheers us up, and on the people whose business it is to keep us cheerful. They produce the 'ooh-ahs' of those whose fancy is tickled by the exploits of celebrities, whether those are footballers or fashion models. With that can go cynicism about politics and politicians. Politicians can do with healthy scepticism, but there is a crucial difference between that and corrosive endless cynicism.

Great and Terrible Happenings

The Cold War and After

The above picture of our rather confined interest in matters political, no matter how threatening some of them were, has to be much qualified. By the Cold War. By now it is almost two decades since the more obvious threat, from the Soviet Union, was lifted. That is, of course, the threat of nuclear war, which reached a dreadful peak roughly midway in the Cold War, with the Cuban Missile Crisis of 1962. We know now that at that point the world had come quite close to the brink of destruction. The threat still exists, though more submerged. Meanwhile, the number of nations capable of waging that kind of war has steadily increased. But nowadays few of us are greatly aware of that. The ever-present Soviet threat has, more or less, gone away and most newly married people hardly know that it ever existed. Yet for more than four decades it hung above us; and for those bringing up children it could be felt as a constant threat. One wife of a professor, not in any way a congenital worrier, confessed that she never settled down to sleep without wondering whether her four children would survive to grow, marry and have children as she had. On some evenings, before driving to my adult class, I had time to bathe the children. Every time this happened it crossed my mind to wonder whether I would see them again. For those, relatively few, who saw the film *The War Game*, the likely effects of a nuclear strike shown there, were as of something which might well happen any day. And of course we had the pictures of the atom bombs on Japan always before us. If we had taken them in. This threat, this fear, lasted, then, for almost half a century and like a curse hung over those who recognized it.

And yet, all the time and somewhere at the back of our minds, many of us did not really believe that the worst could happen. We sort of half assumed that we each and all had a kind of charmed collective life, that things would turn out for the best. Two entirely conflicting assumptions coexisted in the one mind.

How odd it is to recall that, in no more than a decade and a half after the war's end, and thus well into that hung-over, that constantly threatened, period of more than four decades, we embarked on the Swinging Sixties, which the mass media assured us marked the end of wartime austerity and its attendant restrictions. As though that was all that was necessary for us to throw off everything that stopped our lives from being one long matter of fun and games. For millions of people it seemed as though the war had never happened or had had no aftermath. One can, as I have done, blame much on the mass media for all this. But in the end they follow trends or do their best to smell out the way those are leading. Most young people were ready for the Swinging Sixties and it must sound churlish to criticize them. Yet understanding 'the young' can soon turn into soft patronage, and ignores the power of the persuaders to encourage young people to accept the role of cultural helots. It was at this point that we first truly felt that we belonged to an older generation.

One needs to recognize that most citizens of modern, 'developed' democracies such as ours are not fully aware of the great events of their time, the good and the bad; unless they become directly involved in them, as agents or victims. Obviously, this was true in earlier periods, but the reasons for unresponsiveness, then for non-participation, are plain. Most of the population were expected to work, not think, and were not trained to do that. Even up to the past century some of those attitudes held – and hold today, with very many people. In the mid-twentieth century almost all my relatives, being working class, had had little education. More, to what still seems now a remarkable degree, my older relatives assumed that political opinions were not for them. This was less because they felt ill-equipped than because they assumed that 'those in charge' saw to it that the lower orders were kept in their place. I do not remember any one of them voting. There were, at all times, some exceptions. It is a weakness of many far-Left thinkers that they concentrate on that minority and do not sufficiently try to understand the pressures which lead the silent majority to be just that: silent.

Even today, a great many people who left school at 16 cannot spell or count accurately. Estimates of the percentage of those who are functionally illiterate vary between 12 and 16 per cent; and many older people are still stuck at that point. Some readers criticized my *The Uses of Literacy* because it made so many working-class people seem 'politically passive'; they were, and to an unhappy extent, many still are. Until that situation is recognized as a challenge, some active Labourites will be one-eyed.

To turn back and insist for a moment. Modern mass communications are astonishingly sophisticated and most of them make their own judgements on what they will communicate, influenced of course by evidence of existing taste; but not entirely – they have their own commercial and political agenda which they are adept at marrying with existing tastes. These judgements tend to be inherently narrow and narrowing. Marcuse's 'repressive tolerance' – by which certain 'unacceptable', 'intolerable', opinions are allowed, simply so as to show how tolerant the particular society or organ of communication is – hardly applies. it belongs higher up the educational ladder. The 'moral cohesion' of such a society hardly exists; it cannot usefully contain both the consciously considered and the unconsciously absorbed; it is fractured.

—

In such a society, to what group do people such as ourselves now belong? If the previous label about being *Guardian* readers and all that then went with it is no longer quite applicable? Where can one find a fitting label? Clearly, we no longer follow the habits of one class (working class for me, lower-middle class for my wife). But some of those older habits, like a snail's trail or surfacing porpoises, do show themselves from time to time. Of course, we could not call ourselves 'middle class'; that would carry too much incidental baggage, even though our income might qualify us for a middle-class tag; but so would that of many people who differ from us in all sorts of other ways. We enjoyed and learned a lot from Michael Young's *The Rise of the Meritocracy*, but would not call ourselves meritocrats; meritocrats tend to be too technological and probably too status-conscious and *arriviste*, too much at ease in the emerging society. We like to think of ourselves as being outside available labels, whilst casting a critical eye on all of them. It does seem likely that a largish part of society is indeed becoming meritocratic at different levels; and some meritocrats inevitably and happily embrace capitalism. We are partly declassed ourselves, but in many of our affiliations remember and respect our origins. We are therefore not altogether 'classless'. We are part of a body, through education a growing body, somewhere in between the other labellings, all of which we reject because none of them adequately reflects our state.

Among some of our cultural forebears or influences were Hardy's Jude and Forster's Leonard Bast. We are, as we ought to be, more self-aware than were either of those, or higher education would have failed. We had had the education they longed for, are well paid, economically and socially more confident, even if we haven't yet found a label for ourselves. If we grumbled, as we and others did, we told ourselves that we did so chiefly on behalf of others, becalmed in mass culture. There are clear elements of self-regard in that claim. We were part not of a class in the traditional sense but of a group brought together by character and social climate, the latter providing most importantly those large-scale educational changes.

Old and Newer Elements

There is another major force in this 'democratic' society, one so far hardly mentioned directly but certainly demanding mention: capitalism. Capitalism is so far woven into almost all social and individual processes that it seems irredeemable; as it probably is, short of revolution and that is not likely. But it is essential for much of its practice to be at all times not simply accepted but resisted. Michael Heseltine, of all people, declared that 'The market has no morality'. That looks and is in a simple sense true. But look and listen further and you realize that in their complete open-eyed confidence the marketers do have a morality and a strong one. The belief in the rightness of the capitalist ethos for the needs of both society and individuals has become so all-embracing that it acts in itself as a satisfying form of morality. Its proponents exude, under the drive of greed, an unabashed 'moral' drive. Morality has been subconsciously redefined. The market gives them a guilt-free conscience.

—

So now, as we move fully into the new century, there is a much more generally diffused prosperity but, predictably, less active political interest, especially among most 'average' young people and others who have allowed themselves to fall out of any engagement with society;

33

though a few have moved towards the British National Party, and most of those early middle-aged. From those of whom little is expected, little will come. The contrast with, for example, political consciousness among many working-class people in the mid-nineteenth century is striking. More striking than helpful; they had much more evident disadvantages to oppose. Today, not so much disadvantages as disabling agents are all around us.

Low-level chauvinism is still alive at some executive and professional levels. Whilst working at UNESCO in Paris I had two passports, one British, the other from the United Nations; both valid. On visits to England, I normally used the British passport. But one day the UN passport was handier so I offered it. A surly Immigration Officer did not, or pretended not to, recognize it. So I offered the British passport. 'What do yer mean, offering that other thing when you have a *British* passport?' he snarled. Is the Immigration Service attractive to such people?

So what might have been and might still be done to help bring about a more 'civil' society? Two movements, each apparently by now past its peak, were very active for some time: feminism and political correctness.

Filtering down and widely, feminism has much to show to its credit. As to language, feminism and political correctness often shake hands. A lot in everyday language was or could be taken as lowering to women. There was not a handy salutation which did not suggest either a woman's married or pre-married status. Hence the adoption of the rather muzzy 'Ms', which indicates neither of those, but simply 'a woman'. General descriptive writing often appeared to assume that its audience was entirely made up of men. And so on; there was room for change. And feminism has naturally concerned itself far more widely than simply with language. Women have come nearer their proper place in society as a whole; not as much as its leading agents would like, but the change is in train. Look for a start at the upper ranks of the BBC. Not that many men have noticed, as we may judge from the legal arguments, by professional women for their rights, which regularly appear in the press. But wider and more persuasive issues, such as the mass media's treatment of women, have not figured deeply in feminism's discussions.

My wife was once criticized for staying at home instead of expressing her independence by getting a job. She had, after all the children were at school, taken a lectureship in a Teacher Training College. She gave it up because, as she explained, she enjoyed more being at the centre of the very busy life of home, children and husband. That whole argument is, of course, rather generationally driven. A younger woman might think that explanation more of an excuse than a justification.

Many thousands of women are, we all know if we visit supermarkets, working today. Presumably, most are drawn from the working and lower-middle classes; and most seem cheerful in their work. It can be part time, provide company outside the house, money for foreign holidays and the like. It would be interesting to know how many husbands take up some housework, now that for at least some of their time many wives are also out at work.

Much the same can be said about the thrust of political correctness. Basically, it is saying valuable things, especially about the way language can hide prejudice of all kinds. It has been particularly effective in pinpointing the insensitivity of much language about disability (a word not accepted). Most of us might well support the elimination of 'lunatic' or a few others. But too many of political correctness's supporters have revealed cloth ears, attacked harmless words by mistaken interpretation and proposed others which are insensitive. Sometimes one is reminded of the old joke: 'Rightly is they called pigs', where the word itself is not sullied but has taken colouring from prejudice about the animal; a sort of reverse dismissal. Is 'differently abled' an improvement on 'disabled'? I think not. The old word did not necessarily suggest that the person described could do nothing at all.

I once had to choose one young woman from several to speak to camera. The man in charge of their group asked me why I had 'passed over' one young woman; I replied that she had been 'rather slow' in saying what she meant. My wording was deliberately emollient; I avoided saying that the girl had been almost inarticulate. The man in charge replied, apropos 'rather slow': 'We don't use that kind of language around here.' Perhaps I should have said that we had tossed up for the single place.

In his gnomic *Five Moral Pieces*, Umberto Eco was right to say of the politically correct that sometimes: 'they work on the letter at the expense of the spirit.' Like feminism, political correctness, whilst often full of fire and fury, paid hardly any searching attention to the many slightly disguised, not quite indirect, but extremely important forces at work today; especially in attitudes towards women and in the corruption of language.

I did not recognize – know about – homosexuality until I was well over 20, and lesbianism years after that. We owe a debt to both feminism and political correctness that both are more in the open today; and freed from automatic censure – except, no doubt, in many pub bar conversations. In those and similar groupings, racist, anti-immigration assertions and those in favour of capital punishment are still common. There has been little enlightenment there, for all our expenditure on education.

—

What else might work towards a more articulate democracy? Education? H. G. Wells was confident of its primary role. In *The Outline of History*, just after the end of the First World War, he insisted that: 'Human history becomes more and more a race between education and catastrophe.' How innocent that seems today. Would that there were so direct a connection. Some of the architects of the Holocaust were both highly intelligent and well educated. So are some of the more active racists in 'advanced' societies today. Yet still one hopes and can glean some evidence that 'a good education' can guide some minds towards a humane maturing. For others it does not do that. To be made at least to begin to work, it must encourage both a critical spirit (skill at debunking) brought to bear on both ourselves and our society; and imaginative sensitivity. For developing the latter, good literature is paramount; it works indirectly, as it should.

What else might help? Not preaching, not today; nor political haranguing. The quiet and consistent example given by family and friends? Yes, to some degree. That can be one of the best influences. Of course, many families inculcate the opposite.

There can be no kind of converted mass audience; that would be against the nature of what one is arguing. 'Fit audience though few'? To some extent, yes, so long as that does not sound and become smug. A less hopeful description would be simply: 'a very small audience'. But probably one that is not single-class bound, or so it seems from letters I receive; expansion there should be an aim of us all.

One has simply to go on and on, in all sorts of different ways.

This chapter has dealt mainly with acts-and-facts, in a rapid two-dimensional picture of the last three-quarters of a century. We now move on to the attempt to put more 'body' into some of those events. So the coming chapters, until the last one, look at family life, the intellectual life, belief and morals, the cardinal importance of words to our understanding of the self and of society, and the power of memory as life goes on. Of course, there were other possible subjects, but these above all demanded to be looked at – at this time, by this old man.

Chapter 3

Mainly Family Matters

It may be that through habit these do best,
Coming to the water clumsily undressed
Yearly; teaching their children by a sort
Of clowning; helping the old, too, as they ought.

(Philip Larkin, '*To the Sea*')

Philip Larkin's lovely, yearning poem calls up all-embracing perspectives, those of the family and its many holds, big and small.

As I said earlier, after three years abroad for me, Mary and I met in summer 1945. Only for a week, then another year back in Italy; demobilization – and family life began.

Settling In

I have also said earlier that for me the greatest gain of all has been the arrival at a sense of family; perhaps not surprisingly, given that our original family was broken apart during childhood. I went then to relatives in a family of five, mixed adults by age and sex. It was mixed-up as well as mixed, and often at war; but there was love there for the lad of 8 who had unexpectedly joined them. My brother and sister went to other relatives. Yet the love was, had to be, different from that given by parents to their children in an unbroken family home.

Marriage and family compose the new and permanent relationship which should see you to the grave. You are no longer solitary, but a lifelong member of a small, entirely and always, connected group. It gives a sense of secure belonging through your attempts at constant care for the others and their constant awareness of you. All now form unique parts of 'us'. Until their marriages. Then, the patterns of feelings change but do not dissolve; they undergo sea changes.

What would it have felt like to be married but childless? The marriage would still have been stable, but the loss for both of you immeasurable. We have had three children. What would it have felt like if one had died or turned out badly? A death would of course have been irreparable. Towards one who had turned out badly the sense of responsibility, of commitment, would have remained and indeed been enhanced, brought more to the daily surface. Nothing, it seems, could actually break the ties. One reads of children who have been 'disowned' by their parents and can hardly imagine the feeling of dislocation; finding it difficult to believe that such a break can actually happen, and be maintained.

Among the memories which stay most firmly in our minds is that of the oldest turning to his mother, at about 4, and asking: 'Shall I be happy all the days?' Almost heartbreaking. It made her want to hold him tight, for ever.

Our children seem to have 'turned out well' in their ways of going on. I use that old-fashioned phrase, in the inverted commas, to steer clear of others which might sound worldly or, worse, self-congratulatory.

Naturally, these interconnectings also embrace the generation before our own. The sight of a granddaughter, looking intense as she is taught to knit by her grandmother, is only one which has a strong typical quality.

Another three-generational moment is as clear now as it was almost fifty years ago. After a year in America, we sailed back and went straight to my wife's parents near Manchester. She was their only child. The front door opened to the two parents and children of 11, 9 and 5. Unadulterated joy was shared by all. The whole scene was like a portrait of familial belonging, of complete happiness. The grandparents, being Northern, undemonstrative lower-middle class, would not have actually uttered such flowery thoughts. The expressions on their faces, their whole bearing, said it all; without it being said at all.

So you see – watch – your children grow up until they are no longer children; and you still watch, without intervening, until they are parents themselves. And after; the intertwinings cannot be unravelled for the rest of your lives. In the course of things your own ages soon begin to seem irrelevant.

Interlude – Korean Preparations

In the early 1950s I was recalled, in case of need in the Korean operations, for a fortnight's retraining in West Wales. I was seen off at Paragon Station, Hull, by a pregnant wife, small son and smaller daughter. The guns and instruments were no different from those we had trained on a decade before. The officers, too, seamlessly renewed their old customs, though one of them, a barrister, made good use of the greater peacetime possibilities; he billeted his 'floozie' at a nearby hotel, so that their sex life was not interrupted.

My first book came out at that time. I heard a review on the Third Programme at Sunday midday, tucked with a large portable radio under the drinks table in the Officers' Mess. Above, the officers' habitual weekend party was noisily going on, all of them amused that 'The Prof.' was pursuing his odd business down below.

I returned to home and work, with no notion of how near I had come to being recalled for active service. The two weeks had been a small, rather amateurish, break or bump, and soon sank deep into the memory. Almost all of us, it had become plain, had turned into thorough civilians in the half-decade since demobilization.

Back to Family Life

Behind all we simply call 'family life', as though its character is easily and wholly captured within that or any other simple phrase, there goes on – unless the members fall into ultimately divisive disagreements – that complex, subtle interplay of different characters through which each is all the time required over the years to learn how to live with the others. First, the parents have to learn, sensibly or insensibly, to adjust to one another, what to say and what not to say, what to do and what not to do. This at the same time as both are trying to be aware of the constant and differing developments of their children and where, if anywhere, they might themselves properly intervene. It is easier to describe these needs than to meet them in full. It is all a constant process whose complexities are only recognized retrospectively, if at all. It is easiest of all either to make these duties smothering to the children or off-putting to friends and neighbours, who react against what can seem like excessively inward-looking, family near obsessiveness.

Obviously, the best pattern is likely to be found by families whose members learn to make allowances, to show tolerance not only to one another but to those outside their ring. Obviously again, and though we cannot ourselves claim total success in all this, we can claim that we tried hard. Looking around, one sees some who did better and some who did worse. Where it does work, one notices a profound everydayness. Wordsworth captured the beauty of this ordinariness, in 'The Character of the Happy Warrior', where he celebrates: 'The common strife / Or mild concerns of ordinary life / A constant influence, a peculiar grace'.

So much for the gain from a sense of belonging as I have experienced it. It would be difficult, and probably unfair in the outcome, to write about the sense of non-belonging in others. But a certain scene comes to mind in which the participants, for all I know, may most of them happily belong somewhere. But in this group they are for the time being huddled, isolated; and do not individually belong. So I use the group allegorically, to suggest what a condition of non-belonging, if it has a physical face, may look like. And it is, after all, a scene created by modern life (though early army life comes near it); mass urinals are typical of the motorways.

The scene is one of those very large urinals on a motorway during a busy weekend morning; full of men jostling and pushing towards the stalls, almost all of them silent, having adopted the face for the occasion – slightly downturned, eyes unfocused, switched off, no expression, unless it is the 'out of connection' expression; a kind of face 'to meet the faces that you meet'. All engrossed in being able to empty their bladders and get out as quickly as they came in. All on the move. All strangers to one another unless an acquaintance suddenly appears, when the eyes momentarily switch on.

A quick flip of the penis to remove drops, a quick zipping up, and for some an equally quick splash in the handbasin.

These are brief suspended moments in what is often a long day which is, in the mind, mainly a prolonged ribbon of road eating up measured but unremarkable time; until at the end of the journey family or friends help you to switch on expressions, reality, again.

A Family Affair: The State Visit to Birmingham

Deeply familial was the, as it were, State Visit to Birmingham of my two very elderly aunts, in the late-1960s. They had been part of my Grandma's household in which I grew up, from 8 to 18. This late occasion was a sort of tribute – and treat – to and for them; several broad hints had inspired it, and eventually it was happily arranged. As expected, it turned out to be a mixture of warmth, pathos, near bad temper and high comedy, since they could be edgy towards each other. The older one could be bossy towards anyone in her whole world. She was a phenomenon of quick-firing assaults. If she had met the Pope she would have 'straightened his jacket all right'; perhaps for misusing women, the nuns who were 'expected to wait on him hand and foot'. Catching sight through an open doorway of our daughter's untidy bedroom, she declared fiercely and incontrovertibly that untidy teenagers always 'landed up as sluts'.

Both aunts were extremely proud of 'where I'd got to', without fully understanding it. That had begun when they had first seen my name 'in the papers'. To them that could only mean one of two things: crime or achievement. I had at Leeds University gained the only first-class degree in English Literature that year, and that appeared in the local paper's annual lists.

The older of the aunts, whilst recognizing that I was 'bright', had been convinced since my adolescence that I worked too hard and would eventually 'do myself a damage'. As the years passed and I made a few appearances on television she uttered the same warning on each occasion: 'Ooh, you did look tired. You'd better take more care.'

By now, though, I was a professor, living in a large Victorian detached house in Birmingham's nineteenth-century, middle-class district of Edgbaston, half a mile from the university. All this was very impressive, and hard for them to assimilate. Both aunts were used to working-class streets, though not to council estates. In later life one of them had even moved up with a woman friend, now dead, to an inexpensive modern semi in Morecambe, that favourite retirement home for Leeds's respectable working-class and, more, lower-middle class people. Earlier, we had all lived in a terrace house. Then, for me, university, the army and academic life, which had eventually seen me married with three children; making a gradual procession up the academic ladder, and being given a certain amount of public repute.

Every year, during the various holidays, we had called on the aunts and other relatives separately and regularly, but few had been to our succession of increasingly distant homes. As I have said, the idea of a visit from those two aunts sort of percolated as an opportunity they would greatly value, and came to have something of the force of a Royal Command. They badly wanted to see where I had 'landed up' before, as they might have said, 'it was too late'.

By then they were both in their seventies and did not travel easily. They had aged into the shapeless but corset-reinforced and rather unsteady figures common among working-class women of their generation. 'Ooh, me feet are killing me', was a frequent announcement. Loosening the corset had to be a more unobtrusive operation.

The visit was precisely prepared. They were collected at New Street Station and driven to a house which startled them. I think it had been built for a maker of nails and was spacious but hardly a treat for the eyes: three cellars, four attics, six bedrooms and two-storeyed separate brick quarters for the coach and coachman. £10,000 for a forty-year lease (in 1962).

'Ooh!', said one, and 'Well, I never!', said the other. No doubt their minds flew straight back to the boy of all those years ago in Hunslet. Then they settled in easily for a few days, enjoying the busy and curious life around them, the evening meals preceded by a sherry or stout; and much reminiscence: 'Ah say, Richard, do you remember that time when... .', followed by an anecdote as risky as the presence of the disapproving sister would allow. Luckily, she went to bed first, though always with a 'Now don't you hang around much longer, Lil', to her younger sibling.

The Sound of Music was showing just down the road. That captivated them and became the crown of the visit, or like a cherry on top of a large fancy cake. With the rest of the visit, it helped gather together and confirm their pride in the nephew whose success seemed 'quite beyond' them, but was cherished. One could easily imagine the tales they would tell when they were back in Leeds.

In its way, that visit was one kind of payment of dues, a sort of thank-you occasion bringing together over the years memories and thoughts of Time and Family and Change, all mixed but also in a sense all one.

Neighbours, Friends and Others

We have been lucky; wherever we went we found good neighbours. This is always backed by that recognized, long-standing English tradition.

We have also been blessed with good friends; not many, but that is right. Dues to be paid on both sides need regular attention. Many confuse acquaintances with friends, which reduces, lightens, the idea of friendship. Three of our friends are still alive, still practising warmth and aiming at mutual honesty rather than mutual back-scratching.

We have had and have still a fairly wide range of acquaintances; but, again, not too wide. Some people collect acquaintances like cigarette cards; and as lightly.

An oddity, which I only recognized late, though I am reminded that Freud observed it: some people seem to dislike you by nature. I do not mean those who, from time to time, are professionally jealous; one is bound to meet those along the way. I mean people who at first glance – and perhaps on first hearing – thereafter show, by looks and even perhaps in words, that they have 'taken against you on sight'; so that you know there is nothing to be done except to withdraw. I have only noticed two or three people of this kind – one was in a class of Polish students, another in a group of librarians, the third across a committee table – but am sure that natural alienation exists and is not, in this instance, an emanation of my own thin skin. It seems more like an instinctive reaction, as though to them you give off an off-putting smell. Perhaps it is to be seen as the opposite of 'falling in love'. 'Dropping into dislike'.

The Supremacy of Women

Women are supreme to men because they can give birth. Men contribute to the process, of course; they supply the spark which initiates it, and their genes are passed on. After that, their work is done until they begin to help, or not, with the development of the child.

I put this obvious matter so nakedly and simply because its astonishing nature has only lately occurred to me – a grandfather! – with its full force. To open your legs and encourage a new being to slide down that otherwise rather mundane channel, complete with toenails and fingernails and all else, to hear that first human cry; all this after the homunculus has grown quietly inside you for a few months – at whatever age it comes home to men, this event should be absorbed in its full remarkableness. No wonder so many women are eager to have that often very painful experience. I would have been eager. In fact, born again, I wouldn't mind being a woman.

Nothing a man can do equals that phenomenon. No wonder that so many men, villainous or virtuous, love their mother with a special aboriginal love, give her pride of place in their emotional universe. Thugs will weep over their double Scotches at the bar in response to a sentimental, mother-fixated, song. And go home and, if they feel like it, beat up their wives; who come second, if that. Women love their mothers too, but differently; as co-conspirators. Their talk together is different, they see the world differently, with a stronger sense of the need for preservation.

Lovely Old Faces

A face to lose youth for, to occupy age
With the dream of, meet death with.
(Browning, 'A Likeness')

The loveliest faces are old, especially those of women; faces fed with many memories, faces which have endured. Seeing some old woman's or old man's face you find yourself wondering how they must have looked when they were young. What kind of beauty did they have then, for there are very many kinds? Better perhaps to put aside 'beauty' for a moment and speak simply of 'attraction' or, at a pinch, of 'allure'; of qualities which need not be called 'beauty' in any usually recognized sense, but are more than that.

Few are not blessed in youth. In their twenties, what attracted would-be lovers? Not, usually, the standard elements looked for in models. But those with certain differences; an unusual element – sometimes in the bone structure of the face, the slight unusualness of the eyes, a small difference in the set of the mouth, the hair – especially when it is drawn back over the ears – the height of the forehead, and the combination of all or some of those; that is, the almost numinous expression – thoughtful, lost, or happy to confront life – which gathers the rest together. 'Oh God, she has a lovely face…'

There is endless interest in wondering what came together to attract, all those years ago; and which of those elements can, in spite of the depredations of time, still be hinted at, or even surpassed, in old age.

The enquiry can be reversed. How are that very attractive young woman or man going to look when they are old? What, if anything, will remain of the early beauty? 'She hasn't worn well' used to be a common and harsh judgement, and perhaps still is.

The pressures of the time have narrowed the accepted meanings of 'beauty', as especially in the Miss World contests. It is of the essence of those that they avoid alluring quirks, which will not appeal to all, but seek some standard pattern or patterns. The effect is therefore in a sense two-dimensional; it suggests no hinterland or, latterly, only a suitable hinterland invented by the Public Relations team: 'I would like to do some useful voluntary work; and I like reading, especially of historical novels.' You bet. You can't really imagine living next door to one and catching sight of her without make-up and in a working pinafore. You don't have to; this is a shadow world, which has to suggest more than it can ever deliver; or would wish to. Hence the popular, slightly sulky-remote expression which suggests at once both 'Come hither' and 'Keep off the grass'.

That is the point, if it hasn't been reached before, that you acknowledge with a happy sense of release, that true beauty defies age, that age can have its own kind of beauty, that all ages on the way can have their own beauty, with which the possessor and the observer can grow old. As, particularly, in those lovely lived-through faces of some old women.

I saw it in my Grandma who 'brought me up'; long after having ten children of her own, some already dead; the etched-in lines on her face recorded that story.

In 'The Model', Auden celebrated one such: 'She survived whatever happened; she forgave; she became.' In 'Old Woman', Joseph Campbell found that: 'As a white candle / In a holy place / So is the beauty / Of an aged face'. Donne caps Auden's twentieth-century intellectual summing-up and Campbell's Irish religious summing-up, in 'The Autumnal': 'No spring nor summer beauty hath such grace, / As I have seen in one autumnal face'. Browning yearned before a face loved through time, as in the epigraph at the head of this section.

One muses, with Auden, as to how they arrived at such faces. Perhaps their expressions when old emerged from their kinds of early beauty, aided by sustained courage, humour and tolerance even towards the self; but no pettiness. Endurance, to live through all that comes to you without final depression or dismay; for, to remember Auden again, at that age a touch of despair could be 'instantaneously fatal'.

Chapter 4

Uncertainties and After

Odd Hang-ups

Whether an early thinness of skin was a fact of nature or, perhaps more likely, the result of nurture, or a mixture of both, I simply do not know. I look at it here because it may interest, especially, anyone who also had some of this disposition when young. A few decades after its prime, it now seems reduced in me. I put this change down, chiefly, to that blessed development in the mind, and so of the self, which education can encourage.

As to the earlier sense of insecurity, I suppose there was, added to the fact of being poorer than most youths, my small stature and rather soppy-sounding lisp. At the back of my head, though never put into words, was sometimes the image of a ring of smiling, talking men and women all of average height or above and well dressed, assured – and a little man outside the ring, seeking to prise apart the legs of one big chap so as to become a member of the circle; and ready with some intriguing anecdote. Slightly Chaplinesque. The tales had early become something of a compensation. Such an image is usually deceptive, if left unaccompanied. I could also be cocky, sensing that at any rate I could talk faster than many I subsequently met.

By the sixth form at grammar school an interest in small social differences grew. As when I was taken to tea by classmates and, though this happened only rarely, the boy's mother – having been told of my family circumstances – could not prevent herself from being slightly patronizing; an attitude rather nervously enhanced when she was told that I was 'clever'. One very sensitive boy apologized for his mother's behaviour. I had my eye also on just what food they provided and on how adequate it was; a few such visits produced a little cultural-comparative paragraph in the mind.

Much later, after my *The Uses of Literacy* was published, some people used to ask me, quite simply: 'What College were you at?' Apparently, anyone who had written a successful book could not have been educated at a provincial university. That little revelation of academic class-consciousness occurs less often nowadays.

To their credit, some 'superior persons' refused to play that game. On one occasion a rather large and grand professor – years before I reached that rank – known to think well of himself, tried to divert the Director-General of the BBC from a conversation with me by interrupting over my shoulder with a new topic. Hugh Greene must have been used to that sort of ploy, and ignored him. Later, the professor, who seemed to have decided that anyone the DG addressed by his first name must be 'someone', came over to talk to me. A trivial incident, but in those days quite common; and indicative. And, on second thoughts, not trivial; rude and foolish, rather.

One result of all this is the disinclination to be much of a mixer. Which is probably a pity. Nor, though I have 'risen' in my profession, do I have much ambition. I prefer to go on going on and perhaps be taken by surprise. Perhaps some others might call that a disguised form of ambition.

One result of the disinclination to mix-and-mingle seems emotionally connected, in reverse as it were, with that urge to be accepted which was described earlier. I have said that I do not fully understand all this – 'shyness', I have to call it. I have let go several opportunities to meet very important people, all now dead, whom I greatly admired. But 'shyness' does duty for want of a more accurate word. Among other influences, the attitude seems to arise from the remaining sense that though I have had to work hard, as have so many others, to arrive wherever I now am, intellectually as well as socially, I still do not feel I quite belong there. Many other people have made that journey and don't make such a meal of the process.

There was, I now remember, a reverse incident of the above kind which also reflects on my hang-ups but, more importantly, shows the admirable freedom of another person.

I was at a literary reception in the magnificent royal Banqueting Rooms in Whitehall. I seemed to know no one and was standing alone against a wall. I looked up and saw Iris Murdoch at the opposite wall, also alone. I had met her and John Bayley at a literary conference in Denmark about thirty years before. I did not go across to greet her, for reasons which will be obvious by now, and because I assumed that so celebrated a writer would not be alone for long.

She looked across, saw me and at once walked across the room to where I stood. 'Do you remember me?', she asked. 'We met in Denmark some years ago.' That fine gesture implicitly rebuked me.

The Ever-handy Notebook

I have for years carried around with me, and put at my bedside each night, a small notebook; and would not be without it. I would, as the saying is, feel naked then. I seem to remember that Milton, being blind, called one of his daughters to his bedside, to take down sudden thoughts. My notebook has the same purpose, and when morning comes I am grateful for the jogs to memory. Unfortunately, about half the notes are undecipherable. There are moments when a thought occurs but I feel loath to sit up and reach for the pad; I trust to memory, which almost always lets me down. I knew there had been an interesting thought, but cannot remember what. At other times, a scribble can prompt a small revelation. In addition, by note-taking one is trying to build a hedge against what might be costly forgetfulnesses. If it fails, the sense of loss is greater than if you had not consulted the notebook. Or over-reliance on the book rather than on your own daily memory can have its own costs. Note-taking can be faulty.

As I directly learned. One summer we arranged to meet our younger son at Trieste railway station, late afternoon on a Saturday; he was then in his late teens and joining us directly from a holiday in Greece. Normally, that date would have rested in the mind to be acted upon and then deleted. But I had put it in my notebook – against the Sunday; and it was that I followed, rather than relying on memory. I trusted the notebook; and we turned up 24 hours late. Luckily, our son had guessed I had made some sort of mistake, taken himself back to the Youth Hostel for the night, and then sat down to wait again at the station for most of the next day. It must have been a very worrying wait, all that way from home and no assurance that his guess was accurate. Had we had a breakdown or accident? I can still blush at the memory; and admire his fortitude.

Money

For several decades after the early teens I had a preoccupation with money; not surprisingly, I imagine. At school, would there be money at home to pay for that official school outing? Perhaps, but only with an effort, 'a bit of scrimping'. They didn't want me to seem at a regular disadvantage. Or money for that non-official group's trip to the theatre? Probably not; one couldn't keep up with those other boys. I came not to mind. The household was obviously doing its best but the weekly income simply did not stretch to the increasing demands of grammar-school life. A few others were in the same position so the disappointment was alleviated. That condition of continuous 'scraping', even if it was about only a few shillings, was like a tight belt against unexpected activities and other expenses. I had pocket money, of course, about threepence a week in the really early years. That was enough to go to the Saturday matinée at the Parkfield Picture Palace, again with others in the same boat. A few years later came: 'Is it my turn to buy this round of drinks?' (Much as I would have liked to.) Or: 'Can I overcome the reluctance to be the first to pick up the café bill?' And so on, through university; until I had worked my passage and was released.

I have just remembered a curious but in a way inevitable incident about pocket money. One of the aunts at home worked on a ready-made clothing line near to a woman whose son was in my class at Cockburn High. They tended to be edgily if unconsciously competitive towards each other. 'My Jack (to invent a name) gets a shilling a week pocket money,' said the other woman. Not a bad sum, that. 'So does our Bert,' said my aunt. I didn't. I had at the time sixpence. The conversation soon emerged from the boy, at school. I did not 'let on' the truth to him or mention the incident at home.

Was this concern about money natural to me or a result of circumstances? I like to think it was a product of the latter. As it was for almost all the homes around us. I do not tire of making this point and will do so again. In those homes successive weeks and the wages they brought in, if they were lucky enough to have a 'breadwinner' in work, followed a repetitive pattern of wages-in wages-out, almost to the last penny. The level of ability in handling that determined either just managing or running up a debt, or adding to existing debts. 'Managing' was one of the words constantly in season. No wonder that the one passage in Dickens of which most people knew was Mr Micawber's admonitions on money management.

It is easy to understand how a regular concern about money, for 'making ends meet', seeped down to children as a fact of adult life, even though they may have paid no practical heed to it; not then. You did 'pay heed' if most children you mixed with, of roughly the same age and educational situation, had more than you had. You learned to calculate.

At an early point in my university years I made such a calculation and found that I appeared to have only one shilling (5p a week) left over after paying all dues. Such exercises can be deceptive. I managed at that earlier time, with some help from a couple of charities and some other unsolicited kindnesses. A room in Hall and meals had been paid for in advance. There were few outside demands or costly habits, no visits to a Union Bar or dance or similar activities. I soon learned to cut my coat according to my cloth. On some weekends I allowed myself five cheap cigarettes, Woodbines at sixpence (two and a half pence). Soon, the pipe had become a student fashion and proved to be cheaper even than the cheapest cigarettes. Some of us learned to mix, half and half, an ounce of cheap pipe tobacco with something even cheaper, which smelled of horse fodder and came from an early form of Health Food shop somewhere in the Eastern Counties, St Albans or Bedford or a similar unknown but presumably slightly countrified town. For me, that herbal alteration came from my professor. One day, finding his room full of that strange smell, I was introduced to the mixture. I learned to know his habit of veering between great generosity and tiny economies, of which he tended to be proud because they indicated that he was one up on expensively advertised products. 'Fill your pipe,' he said genially, tossing his pouch over. At that stage I was puzzled about the impulse to make such economies. He had told me that his salary was £900 a year – about £18 a week. One of my uncles was hoping eventually to be 'a five-pound-a-week man'.

My 'girlfriend', as she then was, had ten shillings a week from her father (50p – these comparisons need major translations, of course). If needed, that paid for us both. It provided fish and chips (a penn'orth and a tuppeny each, or one shared) on the way back to our Halls after the university library had closed and all Hall meals had ended. Mary must have known from the start that I was hard up. Our first 'date', my first ever, was to see *Green Pastures* at the city's Paramount Cinema; I think we went Dutch. In general, any extra pounds, from wherever they came, 'made all the difference'.

Almost six years in the army, most of those as an officer, meant that money seemed for the first time not much to concern me, especially overseas. Part of my pay went directly to a home account, against the start of family life on demobilization. We had married in summer 1942, just before the North African invasion. For once, I did not feel hard up; the years in the army were comparatively cushioned.

The old concern came back after demobilization. Not immediately, because of our savings. But we had a baby, and all to buy for it. The savings had gone within a year. University salaries had fallen behind so that the starting figure in 1946 was, if I remember correctly, £350 a year. It hardly needs saying that nevertheless those were good and happy years. But from mid-1947 the matter of money became, if not entirely preoccupying, then an often recurring thought.

It all was, naturally, part of the overall sense of responsibility which having a family brings. More; half-consciously, I did not wish us to drop to the level I had known as a child, though clearly that was not likely even in the early years.

After a while I made another calculation, similar to the one made as an undergraduate, of what came in and what went out. My wife rightly thought it unnecessary but put up with it. It again proved that we had more going out than was coming in. This seemed unlikely so something was probably wrong with the figuring; as before, it was ignored and we did not have to live on bread and dripping or margarine. We have never had an overdraft, or bought anything on hire purchase or had a debt to anyone; or, for that matter, owned shares. We have had a mortgage, unwillingly.

Over the next six years we had two other children. University salaries remained for some time slow to increase; the concern about money, with managing and calculating, substantially remained, increasing as the demands of the family grew. But I began to earn a little from writing and, very occasionally, from lecturing. It is, incidentally, an admirable point of honour in the world of Adult Education at all levels that lectures are unpaid and the cheapest 'mode of transport' to reach them suggested. One West Country group asked me to give them a talk, the date to be decided by the convenience that some other body would be paying for the Hull to London return leg.

The money blight remained longer than it should have done, so that I can still blush at the thought of a few refusals of requests for extra money by the children. If I gave the money, I sometimes accompanied it with a small homily on thrift, living within your means and so on. One of them, in a very friendly way, suggested I might loosen up a bit and 'forget the backstreets of Leeds'. Good for him. Even in those times, though obviously much more easily today, I can revert into a mild prodigality; and, if I have two of anything but need only one, I look around for someone to give the spare to; often a slightly disconcerting gesture to the chosen recipient.

During that time finding the answer to some frequent minor problems brought a mild worry: the size of a tip to a taxi driver or waiter (settled now at 10 per cent or a little more if that seems right); how much to give to charities (these are now extensive), or to a whip-round for some professional cause and so on. I learned to err on the side of generosity and, after the first hiccup, to feel rather pleased with myself.

Above all was care of the family, in itself a proper care but sometimes become not simply a proper care but an improper worry, unnecessarily invasive. The roots are easy to recognize and so, to some extent, to restrain, or to dilute by those occasional brief largesses. Even now, to put on the page this little bit of self-criticism is rather liberating. I should also have said earlier in this bumpy cycle that professional promotions and outside earnings eventually made such niggles otiose.

So by now I have learned to manage this tendency; and, within myself, to reject any accusation of 'meanness'. The inclinations towards that condition were quite strong but not impossibly so, not unmanageable. Directly faced more and more, and helped by that increase in funds, they weakened. It is by now some considerable time since I first happily recognized the continuing decline. Once one relaxes, other, perhaps more natural, impulses take over. A great relief.

—

This constant, often long-standing, interest in money among some people who were, like me, from poor or penny-pinching homes, and who are by now comfortably off, is not much talked about but not uncommon. Obviously, it is most evident among those from poor backgrounds. I have sometimes wondered whether some from comfortably-off but miserly backgrounds often react by spending freely. Not all those who come from poorer backgrounds have learned to subdue money concerns even as much as I have done; and some have not had the benefit of an increasing income. On the other hand, some are by now reasonably well off; and among those one can still occasionally recognize the old restraining habits; as in not picking up before anyone else a joint restaurant bill; or discovering suddenly, but at the critical moment, that nature calls for a trip to the loo. This slight but telling aversion is usually accompanied by a moderately pained but cavalierly defensive air which indicates that they have again weakened, know it, and are prepared to carry it off, even to 'brazen it out'. At the saddest, some such people, aware that they are not paying for the meal, cannot resist selecting dearer items on the à la carte menu; but they are rare; perhaps only four of my acquaintances.

So much for what can usually be thought of as, again, a diffused influence of background; or are there some people by nature 'mean'? Without more evidence, I am inclined to think not, though one person makes that thought wobble. A concomitant quality in some people, whether from poor or prosperous backgrounds, is an excessive fear of being 'diddled', cheated.

I still love bazaars, car-boot sales, all the homes of 'bargains' – and the memory of the old-style Woolworths.

Our first visit to the United States highlighted the impulses behind excessive money-consciousness, and freedom from it. Especially in the giant supermarkets which were then new to us. After the first sense of Aladdin's cave excess, the old puritanical sense of retribution – 'you'll pay for this' – set in. Here in Britain I still enter their doors with a touch of careless anticipation mingled with anticipatory self-reproach at the wrongness of all this excess. Yet I still enjoy going into those hangars – thirty-three, or more, checkouts!

Releases – and Results

Sometimes I have felt released from all the kerfuffle described earlier. On each occasion that was part of a general relief; and on each occasion a minor disaster threatened or followed. The first was at the ticket booth of Glasgow's main railway station during the war. I was going on leave from the regiment for a few days so as to marry before, as I, but not my future wife, knew, we would go overseas. I was entitled to a first-class return ticket to the Cotswolds, received the ticket and turned away – casually letting the ticket drop to the boot-crowded floor. Slap-happy. Anxiety set in after only a few seconds. In that crowd it was impossible to retrieve the ticket. I joined the queue again and bought another.

On another occasion, not long after the ticket incident, I had charge of a troop of about thirty men for a day's exercises in the Scottish countryside. There was to be a break of two hours in the middle of the day. My wife was briefly staying nearby. At the break the men set off for the nearest village; the two of us took a walk. I entirely forgot the two-hour limit until it was impossible to be back at the meeting point on time. I was an hour late. The men didn't mind; it had been more time off for them, and gave the occasion for a few ribald jokes.

The third event most strongly suggested that these instances of amnesia all occurred when I was exceptionally free from care or full of anticipation. Embarking at

Boulogne in 1946 for England and the end of army service we were each, at the bottom of the gangway, and after an identity check, given a small brass disc. That had to be handed in at the top of the gangway. I received my ring and duly let it drop. Without it, I would have missed my boat because enquiries about my identity would have had to be made. I scrabbled between the massed, insistently pushing forward, feet on the steeply sloping gangway over the water – and found the disc. After such incidents I realized better what was meant when some people are described as 'feckless'. In one way I envied such people, so happy-go-lucky, but wondered how they escaped from their surely inevitable succession of misadventures.

All three above events were instances of rare emotional freedom with plainly inspired causes and consequences. A further one – just one – seems in its origins more deeply rooted and was certainly happier, though I cannot satis-factorily explain why. I must have been about 14 and was staying with an aunt a few miles out of Leeds. She lived just on the edge of a small piece of unspoiled woodland. One morning I awoke before anyone else and decided to go for a walk in the woods. The dew was still on the grass and the sun, thin and low, directed a water-colour light through the trees. I had as I walked a feeling of total, unqualified content; I was part of a universe and it was all benign. 'The corn was orient and immortal wheat.' I did not know that lovely passage from Traherne (*Centuries of Meditation*) until some years later, at university, but it captures perfectly my mood on that morning.

Were such moments nurtured by times of exceptional physical health? That might have been the basis of it, but more than that was surely needed – equilibrium within the self perhaps.

Looking again at odd moments through Kilvert's capti-vating *Diary* I came upon another passage, not as spiritual as Traherne's but as true to its experience:

> As I came down from the hill into the valley across the
> golden meadows and along the flower-scented hedges a
> great wave of emotion and happiness stirred and rose up
> within me. I know not why I was so happy, nor what I
> was expecting, but I was in a delirium of joy, it was one
> of the supreme few moments of existence, a deep
> delicious draught from the strong sweet cup of life. It
> came unsought, unbidden, at the meadow style, it was
> one of the flowers of happiness scattered for us and
> found unexpectedly by the wayside of life. It came
> silently, suddenly and went as it came, but it left a long,
> lingering glow and glory behind as it faded slowly like
> a gorgeous sunset, and I shall ever remember the place
> and the time in which such great happiness fell upon me.
> (Monday, 24 May 1875)

Kilvert in his fine, flowery, uplifted sermonizing mood and
mode nevertheless comes over tenderly and well, like the
earnest brother who surprises us all by becoming a vicar,
and a devoted one.

My three or four experiences out of time or in another sort
of time were not as overwhelming as Kilvert's, but they
have served. So has from time to time, indeed often, the
simple sense of cheerfulness. For me, as for Dr Johnson's
acquaintance, cheerfulness would keep breaking in. It is
difficult to know why this takes over; perhaps, again, bodily
well-being or something which has sharply tickled the funny
bone. But it seems deep-set within the personality; it fades,
of course, when something sad grips; but reasserts itself
when that has passed.

I now think, though here I may be over-generalizing
from my own experience, that few people are entirely at
ease with themselves and that those who are tend not to be

the most sensitive. For many of us the overwhelming need is to be able to relax, to settle where one is, not to be for much of the time aware of deficiencies, or of further levels to reach, not to find it easy to loosen up, to be able to *play*, mentally as well as physically. 'Worriters.' Those few born with that liberating capacity or who have acquired it can usually be recognized. They smile easily but not ingratiatingly; they do not seem as though they are trying to prove something (especially about the self); they can live within themselves without being uncommunicative or withdrawn. Their smiles may have a touch of amused irony at the oddities of the world, quirky, unharassed, unobsessed, tolerant, not fretful or straining, not out to prove or to deny any trivial thing; accepting but not succumbing to this life's terms, warts and all. Dennis Enright was one of those who had that wonderful expression; it comes out in his poetry too. Then one wonders whether it had been very hard won.

Chapter 5

Introduction to Intellectual Life

Disinterested intellectual curiosity is the life blood of real civilisation.

(G. M. Trevelyan, Preface to *English Social History*)

Separation by Education

Family experience apart, one of the best benefits I have been offered by this culture and this society is the introduction to the intellectual life, to generalization and its relations to particular things (though I am not much drawn or habituated to the regular use of theory or even of generalization). I have, though, made constant use since adolescence of two abstract words: 'culture' and 'class'. I started playing with both those words at about 16; the second came much more to the front rather later, prompted by the army.

—

Life in the Leeds working class during the twenties and thirties could not be described as of the earth, earthy; that might have served better as a description of village life.

Hunslet was certainly down-to-earth, factual, matter-of-fact; and its vocabulary illustrated that. Verbal exchanges were largely held together, for description and judgement, by well-known apophthegms and favourite single words. This set of verbal tools was not shallow but also not abstract. Most people were not trained to pause so as to generalize, or abstractly to sum up. Yet they could easily within the usual vocabulary point a practical or moral lesson. Abstract attitudes and aptitudes were not what the life of the cobbled streets of a large industrial city needed or encouraged. At this point, I am reminded of some evocative words we used very often but which I suspect were hardly if at all heard outside our class. Such as: 'natter-can' – a consistent natterer or foolish grumbler about trivial things; and 'mardy-arse' – usually but not always of a spoiled child given to moaning and fretting, especially about trifles; and 'sarky', a reduction of 'sarcastic' and more dismissive through its compression.

To move out, to begin to learn how to use the mind enquiringly, was the beginning of a liberation. In early adolescence I found confirmation in what were still, for me, unusual books; such as Trevelyan's *Histories*, one of which is quoted at the head of this chapter. It is not easy to write like that nowadays, to say those kinds of thing in that sort of language.

An early result of these changes was the realization that some apparent folk wisdom, especially some very popular phrases for closure of a conversation, worked by eliding the need for thought. Such as: 'Of course, what they ought to do is'; 'It's as simple as that'; 'They're all after the main chance, when it comes down to it'; and 'If it's good enough for my mates, it's good enough for me.' Naturally, some such phrases are not peculiar to working-class people, or to those who no longer call themselves working class but retain many traditional habits. Some can be heard elsewhere

66

including in the lower-middle class; but they are still very common indeed among working-class people, whether or not still self-identified. Much the same can be said about sayings favoured by the old: 'The young have it easy nowadays'; and 'I don't know what the world is coming to; it wasn't like that in my day.'

What of those who were not given better educational opportunities 'in my day'? Most stayed where they were, though many moved physically, to council estates; a few escaped elsewhere. Traditionally, they tended not to practise what they would call 'hobbies'; rather, they often 'did things in their spare time'. Pigeon-fancying is now very much a minority sport and sounds today like a flat-capped rather romantic occupation; allotments are still popular and have long reached middle-class people. I recently met a taxi driver who bred canaries and showed them nationally, and a railwayman who regularly went to classical concerts at the Royal Festival Hall; but those were exceptions. I also met a taxi driver who swore that Farnham – with its dozens of leisure societies – was 'dead'; he watched telly every night, for several hours; as do a majority in what we still have to call working-class and lower-middle-class areas. A striking example of an exception to this generalization is the growing number, especially since council houses have been for sale, who have gone into Do It Yourself. It is a more mixed picture than, say, fifty years ago; but not as varied as might have been expected, given all the objects and activities now on offer. But of course the pleasures of those more active occupations are outnumbered by the invitations simply to sit and watch.

—

How does one 'get on with' former friends and acquaintances on visits nowadays? Some old friendships can be revived, so that after a short time one can usually meet simply as individuals. But also and inevitably a visitor can, behind and unspoken, see them as *examples* of built-in social and educational limitations. As for them, they see you as something of an outsider from another world, though still – one hopes – as a friend. There are boundaries each recognizes. They know that you cannot now help looking, talking and thinking in a way to which they don't on the whole have access. Skins can be thin on both sides. For the outsider it is important to avoid any hint of blokeishness as a substitute for a real meeting.

To recapitulate: boyhood friends still move largely in the world of the concrete, handling both things which are themselves concrete and others which are not but can be adapted. Their language carries the 'mystery' of their trade. Two men came to look at our television recently. They decided in the end that the problem lay in 'the digi'; they spoke of this to each other throughout the visit, without of course involving me or explaining. It was a small instance of the language of an enclosed profession; and of a certain pride in its use. That settled, they turned to me and, like translators, said: 'Your digital box is faulty.'

Those who are now educated outsiders have been given some hold on another world, that of the generalized and the abstract. The new outsider may wish to retain something of the direct and often lively world of face-to-face tale-telling; whether that happens depends on the ability to straddle, which not all of us possess. To some extent the spectators for professional football do straddle the social classes.

Yet some who have not been given access to the ladders can find their route to those other, non-local, ways of seeing and coming to terms with the world, starting with their own part of society.

Cultural change does not run on entirely narrow and closed lines, but finds different routes for different people. Roughly, educated people may read and discuss with their own kind and through their own kinds of agency. Less educated people have their gatekeepers too, from the popular press to television (not so much radio today, though more articulate and talkative people readily respond to radio's many phone-in programmes), to workplace conversations during breaks. Usually such conversations are not systematically argued but move by implication and fragmented assertion. An exceptionally powerful gatekeeper can bring an issue to the level of sustained argument, even in the workplace; but that is unusual; too much is against that development.

Do those without formal education beyond 16 feel they have been starved of opportunities? Some do, but the majority do not. We have already noted that today many no longer call themselves working class but will not necessarily see themselves as on an upward journey, to the lower middles or the actual middles. More elaborate household goods and a car, perhaps second-hand, do not much change entrenched habits; as they easily recognize.

It would be difficult to assess the number of those who move out, other than through greater educational opportunity, as a proportion of their class of birth. Some of my own relatives have made that journey and are no longer working class in their occupations, habits and leisure pursuits. Nor are they lower-middle class. I do not think they would like to be called middle class; too many off-putting implications there. 'Meritocratic' would simply not fit. I imagine that they do not worry much about such labels, and I do not propose to give them one, just yet. The common claim that 'we are all classless nowadays' is altogether too wide to apply here. And the people we are now talking about do tend, as we have seen, to retain many habits of their original class.

Back, for a moment, to those who have substantially remained working class and still often live in council houses, but by now may have bought them. If they have a

69

car it is almost certainly second or third-hand, but more new ones are appearing; they will still have weekly wages rather than a salary, and retain many other older ways.

For those who have had 'the benefit of a higher education', it is tempting to think that they also now have an enhanced ability to detect the deceptive or phoney all around. In so far as such deceits are based in a sophisticated misuse of logic and language, that may be in general true. Yet we soon learn, if we listen carefully, that many of those with little formal education can develop a well-honed humbug detector working through speech, stance, facial expression, gesture and attitude. Many with higher education, especially in other than analytic subjects (which here may include some forms of the study of literature), may come away from that training with their humbug-detecting abilities undeveloped.

Of common humbug- and cheat-detecting phrases which I most easily recall among working-class people are: 'I wouldn't trust him. He'd cheat you as soon as look at you'; 'A fool and his money are soon parted'; 'There's nowt so queer as folk'; and 'There's none so deaf as those that will not hear.'

Passing Corrections

So much for the gains and losses, which are likely as higher education has its effects. What might be retained? A peculiar sense of neighbourliness? There is neighbourliness in the middle classes and, for all I know, higher up than that. I describe the working-class type of neighbourliness as 'peculiar' because of its main roots. Those are in the need for charity because so many are struggling. Or were. Perhaps today's more widely spread prosperity will wear away that need. The need still exists with force in the 'underclass'; but, there, very few are likely to be able to help each other.

One might say something similar about the sense of tolerance. That, too, may exist in any class. Among working-class people 'live and let live' has long been a cardinal motto. 'Don't rock the boat' is also a necessary injunction; to be submerged would be easy. Again, this may be wearing away, if only because so many people are no longer huddled together in cramped streets. Even so, tolerance can be called for; to reduce hi-fi noise from open windows, or about parking spaces when so many have second-hand cars but no garage or adequate driveway.

I am drawing near to overemphasizing old-style working-class virtues. Obviously, I do this because I long believed that those virtues have not been sufficiently recognized. It was worth recalling one or two of them after describing the likely gains from education which take you out of your class of birth; and because one needs to understand also what one might be lost from the transition and what might best be carried over.

That recalls another long-standing impercipience of mine; that towards the lower-middle class. Common banalities suggest that most middle-class people are deeply conventional, have a cosy language of their own (think of 'hubby'), which was mocked some years ago as 'non-U'. With also, it is generally assumed, only the routine opinions of their kind, unintellectual and unimaginative; a life revolving round the regular – but gentle – habits of home, garden, neighbours, a predictable model of car and predictable leisure pursuits. So one could go on. 'Who sweeps a room as for thy sake' comes in as a reminder here. For, as one looks at the unhappinesses, the miseries, the crimes which visit so many people, much lower-middle-class life begins to have its own honourable character, this day-by-day following of the same modest, unaggressive, perhaps unambitious but faithful path. Being overfocused on the working-class life I knew as a child, it has taken me a long time to notice these qualities.

The Love of Argument

Back to the uprooted. I have already spoken of working-class habits which may remain after higher education has made its changes. Some less obvious habits from that source are not always recognized, especially since they are not likely to be found among politically active working-class people.

Most of the rest do not like 'argumentation'. They shy away from it; it may cause 'a real falling-out', 'bad blood'. It may therefore come as an uneasy surprise, to one from the working class, to see in some highly educated middle-class people a positive taste, even a relish, for disputation.

This first and forcefully came home to me during the war when I met, on a neighbouring gun-site, a Hungarian Jewish intellectual, a thirties refugee who later became the anglicized Sir Andrew Shonfield. I do not mean to imply that he liked quarrelling; though he would do that if he thought a professional issue at stake merited it. Rather, he had a taste for robust argumentation, for the play of muscular debate so highly developed that it seemed at one with his considerable physical powers. Physical and intellectual energies were like a single whole. To me, this was a revelation of a sort even university had not offered.

In general, working-class people think that such behaviour might – another use of the same image – rock the boat to an unacceptable extent. They do not so easily distinguish between a quarrel and an equable argument, and fear that the second may develop into the first; and 'before you know where you are' it's open war. There are of course quarrels, 'rows', fights in working-class homes, but those differ from arguments, sustained or short. Many also tend to acknowledge, wordlessly to know the value of, the peacemaker. I still have the initial disinclination for a quarrel, or even – not admirable – for an intellectual disagreement. But by now I can usually get over that second reaction.

There may still be inside me another legacy of working-class attitudes, perhaps related to the dislike for debate: the mistrust of theory. I said earlier that working-class people are unused to theorizing; that is obvious. I did not mean to imply then that, being educated, I relish it. From training I can recognize and acknowledge and even admire the competent handling of theory, though in a guarded way; but I feel no inclination consistently to pursue it. Or that disinclination may be due to the lack of certain intellectual powers. Perhaps there should be another qualification to the above. I tend to be slightly suspicious of abstract patterns, certainly. But some abstract generalizing words have long intrigued me. For instance, as I noticed earlier, 'culture' and 'class'.

But I have no general theoretical approach of the sort which in other people can produce adherents; instead, only pragmatic observing and assorted conclusions. It now occurs to me that this may be why, unlike a few other writers on culture and society of my generation, I have never attracted an identifiable group of like-minded people; or wanted one.

Two Theoretical Occasions

Different aspects of this disinclination to theorize were brought home to me on two occasions, both inspired from America. The editor of an American literary magazine read an essay of mine, on the impact of literature, and was prompted to invite me to a seminar on the condition of literary studies, which he was organizing at the research and study centre at Bellagio, Italy. All the other participants were Americans, and intellectual high-flyers; in various forms of recondite literary theory. They knew one another from conference after conference in the States and more widely. I was immediately out of my depth and even more of my tastes, having read hardly a one of their books. They were polite but minds did not meet. I do not recall a conversation with more than two or three of them and those were in shallow water. This need not have been rudeness on their part, but a lack of interest in what could only have been regarded by them as, in my paper, a too traditional approach to the study of literature, one which they had given up. They were now opening new ways of reading literature and were engrossed by them. I could have read their books in advance and so been better equipped for the meeting. But I had been invited on the evidence of my entirely untheoretic essay and assumed that would justify my presence. I had no reason to expect that the membership of that colloquium would have been so tightly drawn. They were, within the terms of their strict intellectualism, excited by what they were doing. I did not wish to follow them though I came to recognize some value in what they did.

All in all, it was an intriguing experience. But later I decided that their approach could just as well have been used in other, non-literary contexts; and that indicated its final inadequacy as an approach to literature. Its contribution was limited. It enhanced neither the understanding of the unique nature of literature nor of the experience of reading. It devalued them, reduced a book's wholeness and so its achievement; and, for the reader, narrowed the experience.

—

The other occasion was easier to identify since it crossed the boundaries of two separate disciplines and increased my long-standing doubts about some proponents of one set. Again, an American scholar read an essay of mine, this time in *The Political Quarterly*, and invited me to a conference of academic sociologists, in Washington. It turned out that, as compared with Bellagio, some of the thirty or so sociologists there, and of those some of the more eminent, knew my work and thought it in its own way and even to them interesting, and to some extent useful to their discipline.

My paper to the conference was on 'Cultural Studies'. To some of those present, perhaps to a majority, my approach may have once again seemed at bottom just another form of literary impressionism; but others recognized the value of the approach. The majority clearly held to their own sharply-defined patch and, having read my paper, had from the start consigned me to an aberrant, one-man fringe. That was their silent attitude and response.

I felt like a mongrel among thoroughbred bulldogs. Apart from the very few I have mentioned, these sociologists kept in their own circle, obviously discussing the latest shift of theory. Their common attitude did not seem unfriendly but plainly emerged from the feeling that I was not of their discipline, and that we would have nothing to exchange with one another. This attitude was stronger because they were holding on firmly to a particular definition of that discipline; one which is still often contested.

This ensured that they were, if not hostile, certainly quite uninterested in anything I might say; and a few might well have been consciously antagonistic. For them sociology is absolutely and entirely properly a 'pure science', something which leads to testable truths. It is in the same intellectual category as physics or chemistry. It has nothing to do with, or to learn from, literature or those literary handmaidens, criticism or autobiography or imaginative impressionism, as ways to understanding. Much of their drive was devoted precisely to avoiding that kind of ill or undisciplined, that uncouth, messing around.

They employed concepts of great sophistication. They were enclosed, proud, defensive and above all ever so slightly threatened by one who did not belong to their discipline, and probably would – yes, in fact, did – question their right to call their subject a 'pure science', even though that disinclination was shared by some distinguished sociologists. For the majority in that room, most of them not yet internationally eminent in their discipline, much was at stake: the very reality of their discipline as they defensively and fiercely defined it. The Campus Test was at the back of their minds: were they wholly accepted as members of one of the sciences on their campus? Presumably not always, not everywhere,

My paper was in its turn read to the meeting; and fell as flat as an old, cold kipper. By that time the lack of interest in what this transatlantic visitor might say was obvious. It was as though a group of exceptionally orthodox Roman Catholic priests had been offered a paper on Christian Science. I was an intruder.

Their position illustrated some aspects of scholarship in the USA, though they do occur elsewhere. Sociology is after all a relatively new subject and, as I have already said, its claims to be an exact new science are still being challenged by scholars in both their own and other disciplines. The free, confident and large exponents of it can move within and outside its uncertain boundaries with relative ease. Less secure scholars, especially those spread across that huge continent, in large urban universities, small and remote colleges and all kinds in between, could not easily accept so vague, so academically untethered, a definition of their subject; it left them out in the cold. It had to be made solid, firmly tethered to an undeniably academically acceptable discipline – as one of the new natural sciences. They might have been said to shun with a shudder anything which could not be externally validated (none of Leavis's final and deniable question to a discussion group: 'This is so. Is it not?', for them). They could not relax. They could not go back to their sometimes suspicious colleagues in other disciplines admitting that their academic definition of their subject was still being questioned.

I do not suggest that my paper had had such a direct effect, but it did implicitly suggest that there were other valid ways of studying society. They were unable to reopen their minds to the interest of open skies. Their clinging to the claim of being 'pure scientists' had led to a closure of part of the mind. At this point I always remember a passage by Auden from many years ago, in his essay on Henry James's *The American Scene*. It is as telling as ever:

> In grasping the character of a society, as in judging the character of an individual, no documents, statistics, 'objective' measurements, can ever compete with the single intuitive glance. Intuition may err, for though its judgment is, as Pascal said, only a question of good eyesight, it must be good, for the principles are subtle and numerous, and the omission of one principle leads to error; but documentation, which is useless unless it is complete, *must* err in a field where completeness is impossible.

Michael Oakeshott is briefer: 'Social science is never a science, because [it is] imbued with values and valuative action.' That is exactly the point.

I may have given the impression that I entirely dismiss the efforts of those criticized above. That is not so. I believe their efforts will never reach scientific validity, but they have the right to work as if that is possible and so may arrive nearer that sort of proof; which is useful.

The papers prepared for the meeting were gathered together, to be edited by the man who had invited me to the meeting. I handed in mine, made ready for publication. Some months later I received a letter from a secretary saying merely that the editing of the volume had passed from my sponsor to one who had not exchanged a word with me at the conference. She had been asked to tell me, baldly it seemed, that my paper would no longer be included in the volume of Proceedings. I guess it would have stuck out like a bare-arsed beggar in that company.

The incident reminded me, wryly, of an earlier university occasion. A candidate for admission to read sociology had been advised by her sixth-form teacher to read, in advance and among other books, my *The Uses of Literacy*. The Head of Department, a famous sociological 'number cruncher', interviewed her and asked what books of sociology she had read in preparation for the interview. She included my book above. He discounted that, as a 'coffee-table book'. But she was given a place. The university was Leeds, my own Alma Mater. The book is based on Leeds experience. Not an important fact, but a curious coincidence.

Chapter 6

Self-love, Belief, Morals

Know thyself? If I knew myself, I'd run away.
(Goethe, *Conversations with Eckermann*)

Self-love

It is obvious that we are governed more by our emotions than by reason; and that the cleverer we are the more successfully we can rationalize and to some extent disguise our emotions. Self-love must be the most powerful of our emotions. We do not like to look at ourselves dispassionately, if that is possible. It usually isn't. Thoreau neatly claimed that it is as hard to see oneself as it is to look backward without turning round.

'Love one another.' For most of us that injunction has little force, even though it may be uttered on many religious occasions. There are multiple forms of self-love: self-preservation, self-justification, self-exoneration, self-excusing, self-regard, self-exculpation and many more; it is not surprising that so many labels exist to describe the facets of self-love. That major drive is as often hidden as explicit; so what many call love for another is often diverted self-love.

Nelly Dean in *Wuthering Heights* dourly asserted that we must all be for ourselves in the long run. She was only one in a very long line indeed. I knew a woman, devoutly and explicitly a Christian in all the usual ways, who seemed to have no difficulty in also declaring that: 'First and foremost we must all look after our own when it comes to the crunch. No one else will.' Many millions of Christians would agree with her.

Bacon (*Essays*: 'Of Love') offered his usual economical conclusion: 'The arch-flatterer ... is a man's self.' Nietzsche thought self-love the most vulnerable and at the same time the most unconquerable of qualities: 'He who despises himself nevertheless esteems himself as a self-despiser.' Clang, go the gates. Philip Larkin characteristically said that to ignore self-love is like ignoring gravity.

Here is the main obstacle to our thinking dispassionately of others. That is one of the main and purest of moral impulses, but exceptionally hard to practise, 'when it comes down to it'. Did Captain Oates leave the tent because he was ready to surrender his own life so as to give others a better chance of saving theirs? So we were told, in school. Yet it is an astonishing thought, almost 'against nature', one has first to say in admiration. We would like to think it true; perhaps it was. Unless there is some evidence of which I am ignorant, we will never know for sure. Otherwise, all we have is that laconic last sentence, which can be taken as a deliberate final factual announcement. The simplicity itself may be felt slightly to reinforce the idea that this was indeed an instance of selfless self-sacrifice. Or has it been burnished for public consumption?

For most of us, self-love expresses itself in more mundane ways. It can be a source of hidden sorrow because, as Nietzsche said, at bottom many of us intermittently despise ourselves precisely because of our self-love. Those who do not do that tend not to be very nice to know; and their types of gossip, without their realizing it, expose them.

For most, self-love produces constant anxiety about one's place. So we pick up early, and go on acquiring, multiple signs of where we are and where we should by now like to be, and beyond. The entanglements are immense and affect home, neighbours, friends, professional colleagues, almost everyone we meet.

But some can break out, in particular by an act of charity, no matter how small. E. M. Forster is illuminating here, where he talks of 'rent'. A taxi driver asks for a large sum and, since you think he may be cheating, you are inclined to haggle. But he may be honest and to be accused of cheating might wound him greatly (and may even make him decide that, if that is how people treat him, he might as well act accordingly, i.e., cheat). So you pay what he asks. That is the 'rent' you pay for trust in the idea that some people really are honest and should not have their honesty impugned.

I can remember only one occasion – though I hope there were more which I have forgotten – when I paid 'rent' in Forster's sense. In London, a woman apparently in distress turned to me at a bus stop and said she had lost her purse and did not even have the fare home. It crossed my mind that her story may have been a con; it was not possible to know. I decided to believe her and gave her £5. I expect that some people act in that way more often.

Belief

Leave thou thy sister when she prays.
                    (Tennyson, *In Memoriam*, xxxiii)

Tennyson can sound mawkish above, or rather patronizing to a devout sister. I make use of it here as a warning to atheists and agnostics like myself to treat the urge to believe

with respect. We all know that church and chapel atten-
dances are very low today. Yet many more people, who
probably go to a place of worship only on high days and
holidays, will tell you that they believe. 'It stands to reason'
that there must be someone up there who created the
world. Then morality is given its place: 'And we will all be
judged when we get up there.'

In his lucid *The Loneliness of the Dying*, Norbert Elias
has made the most impressive contemporary statement by
an unbeliever that I have seen:

> Death hides no secret. It opens no door. It is the end of
> a person. What survives is what he or she has given to
> other people, what stays in their memory. If humanity
> disappears, everything that any human being has ever
> done ... including all systems of belief, becomes
> meaningless.

Surprisingly, I find that brave and quite comforting.

I call myself an agnostic for the simplest of reasons, not
as a hedging-bet. To say you are an atheist is to claim an
assurance to which you have no right. How can you know?
You can't. Yet an agnostic may have decided that, though
he cannot say absolutely that there is no God, yet nor can
he find it in his mind or heart to accept that there is such
a Supreme Being.

In his essay on Montaigne, Emerson declared that: 'Belief
consists in accepting the affirmations of the soul; Unbelief in
denying them.' I find no such 'affirmations' in my 'soul' or
mind; and say so dispassionately. Umberto Eco speaks of: 'the
obligatory sense of the holy', which again I do not seem to
have. Kant is easier to nod at, in his claim that mankind is
simply made of crooked timber. Dean Swift, unexpectant as
ever, asserted that some of us have enough religion to make
us hate, but not enough to make us love. That requires

particularly close attention, of a different order from Kant's brief, but stark, statement. That in turn recalls Cardinal Newman's awful statement that, since there is a God, mankind is involved in some terrible aboriginal calamity.

I am neither incredulous nor dismissive about the possibility of such events as the Virgin Birth or the Resurrection. If there were to be an all-powerful Maker of the world and all that is within it, there need be no difficulty for that essence in bringing about those and other miracles. And presumably the thought of many universes harbouring multiple forms of life, all created by one God, can be absorbed also. But perhaps that will become more difficult as discovery follows discovery.

I said above that, for very many, morality flows out of belief, or may flow. Bacon called moral philosophy 'a handmaid to religion'. It reduces, or aims to reduce, self-love. And if we have no religion, where do we find ethical demands or guidance, if we feel the need? How do we cope with what Christians call 'sin' and we can call what we wish, whilst recognizing that we are both talking about much the same thing. Some people speak of 'Natural Ethics', but that seems to answer the question without actually doing so; it simply asserts.

I do not know why, but I have long felt the need to justify ethical actions, for a personal morality; or a taste for moralizing, perhaps one shared with others. In this, I seem something like George Orwell of whom Cyril Connolly neatly said: 'He could not blow his nose without moralising on the state of the handkerchief industry' (*The Sunday Times*). If there is not some sense of morality, let alone of judgement (and, somehow, justice), then life must seem empty, or saved from that only by a succession of ephemeral treats.

The lack is, then, in the need to find an explanation for mankind's manifest failings and also something to explain our compensatory virtues, though not necessarily expecting to reach belief in a benign or just First Cause. The sense of these lacks has not lessened in me and, I would guess, in many others since belief went. I have not found an explanation.

How did that sense arise in the first place? Several people seem to have contributed to its appearance in me. There was unmistakeably the influence of a grandmother who brought me up not as a devout churchgoer (though I did go regularly to Sunday School) but as one who like herself should follow a set of rules which helped make for 'decent' living in challenging circumstances; then the Chapel itself, after I had left Sunday School but still went for a while to Sunday evening services. There were also various people and institutions around me including, surprisingly, the Salem Cycling Club (named after a local Methodist Chapel, where it originated. The ties had long gone) with which I spent many Saturdays during adolescence, discovering the Yorkshire Dales. The Club, though nothing was written, had a set of remarkably suitable ethical rules, such as: help a member and never leave anyone until their problems are solved. That could be explained as only an internal group rule, not as disinterested ethical action. Yet they would not appropriate anything found by the wayside but would hand it in at the nearest police station; nor leave any café without paying though that would often have been easy, nor leave a stranger found in trouble at the roadside. They were not at all smart alecs and gave good lessons to a newcomer.

I also knew at that time a few emerging fly boys already well on the way to discarding all ethical lessons and learning the rules for being 'on the make'.

I gradually became acquainted also with certain writers, in particular novelists – Jane Austen, George Eliot, Thomas Hardy, Joseph Conrad, E. M. Forster and through to Graham Greene – to name the merest few of those who especially illuminated moral dilemmas.

Yet I still sometimes vaguely feel, not think, that there is someone up there, taking notes. I don't *believe* it. If I were able to pursue the question, that pursuit would have to be partly eschatological before it was ethical. I have, I suppose, made plain that I find the ethical tie to a Maker not now acceptable, the terms of that settlement unfair, one-sided. I am asked to believe in a God who, for our ultimate good, created all that we cherish in the world and also all that is cruel and terrible in that world and in us, from murder to wars to earthquakes and tornadoes; and to believe that those enormous contradictions will be resolved in God's good time. I might wish that to be so, but can just as easily imagine a God cruel enough to give us all those capacities to sin, and to visit all those horrors on us, just because he so wills. This is, I recognize, a fairly common position and one to which Roman Catholicism holds what it believes to be a satisfactory answer.

What still remains, 'purely emotionally', but it does seem now and again to try to escape into the area of belief, is an experience which on first recall seems a minor but real adjunct to belief; that is, the force of many hymns. It is very easy to set that aside as 'simply the attraction and power of music', which is to state but not analyse the assertion of a connection. There can be power there which may reinforce belief, after belief has taken place.

One wonders what runs through the mind of a devout Muslim, passing the doors of a great cathedral as such a hymn surges out. Nothing relevant to belief, I guess. It is highly unlikely that many Muslims now living in Britain have been converted to Christianity by the power of its music; or by anything else. For many Primitive Methodists in my boyhood the numerous hymns they knew seemed integral to belief as they felt it.

Are those memorable hymns, even to a Christian, really more significant than other not religiously connected tunes that well up in the mind? Such as 'I dreamt that I dwelt in marble halls', which haunted me for a few days recently, when I heard it on the radio after a long absence. It was instantly succeeded in the memory by a boyhood parody: 'I dreamt I was tickling my father's bald head / With a bottle of sweet oil and a feather / But when I awoke I found it no joke / He was tanning my arse with a leather.'

Courage and Moral Courage

Words are for those with promises to keep.
(Auden, 'Their Lonely Betters')

It is worth repeating here the line from Auden which gives the title and the epigraph to this book as a whole. It echoes throughout, for Auden pinpoints there a main element of moral courage: honesty in our relations with others. Betraying them, we betray ourselves. Rochefoucauld in his *Maxims* neatly widened that when he defined courage as: doing unobserved only what we would do before the world. Kierkegaard was even crisper in observing that we tend to be subjective towards the self, objective towards others; but that the true task is to reverse that order. A good test of this is also our tendency, when we are to blame, to lash out at others, to seek anything which will help us to shrug off hardly bearable guilt. Another is when, in describing weaknesses in others, we half-consciously describe ourselves. Yet another is the warm description of others' virtues, as a secret invitation to have them ascribed to us.

This brings us to the third main theme of this section. If the hold of morality, not reinforced by or inescapably drawn from religious belief, remains, what are among the important tests and arenas for the expression of morality?

I propose a look at various forms of courage. Not simply physical courage but the ability to perform acts of courage in the face of great physical or psychological or emotional danger, or perhaps involving great loss, which may not benefit the doer, but are done, consciously or not, on behalf of others, even of others with whom you are not connected and whom you may not even know. At this point self-love is overridden; that is the first necessity. This I call, unsurprisingly, 'moral courage' and distinguish it from other forms of courage, whether they are at bottom 'interested' and so forms of self-love, or 'blind' acts of daring or 'naked courage' or anything else of those sorts.

When a mother, animal or human, faces death to protect her offspring, is she showing courage? It would be easy to say 'yes'; too easy. She is most likely acting from instinct. That what she is driven to do may result in her own death is not relevant.

We often say that mountain climbers who face death in scaling the most difficult peaks are exhibiting great courage. The word is just about acceptable there, whereas it is not acceptable apropos the mother protecting her young. The climber may fully recognize that death may be the result but decide to take that risk for the thrill of pitting human wits against the dangers posed by a dreadful climb. So a certain definition of 'courage' may be just allowed here; but, for clarity, 'bravery' might be better.

I qualify that acceptance because what is being shown is an entirely personal, an interned, quality; it concerns only the climber. Moral acts should concern someone other than the one person; though those others may not be actual individually known people, but others of 'mankind' now or in the future.

So we approach that finest form of courage: 'moral courage'. The climber is not exhibiting 'moral courage' because that would need someone else or some important idea which is involved with the climb. A complex contrast would be between the climber and a fighter pilot who is willing to lose his life 'so as to protect others'. Explicitly, and always? In some instances, no doubt 'yes'. But the impulses of fighter pilots may be many and often personal. Some embark on their missions for the hell of it. Yeats's poem 'An Irish Airman Foresees his Death' is well worth reading here, for its intricacies of motives, none of them 'patriotic': 'I balanced all, brought all to mind, / The years to come seemed waste of breath, / A waste of breath the years behind / In balance with this life, this death.' As a contrast, the thought of Captain Oates may again be recalled here, as possibly a prime instance of moral courage, the deliberate laying down of one's life for others.

What, then, of courage in battle, of which the highest form is recognized in this country by the award of the Victoria Cross? The citations for these have their own vocabulary, centred on willingness to sacrifice one's own life so as to save the lives of comrades, or to turn the course of a battle; the two will often run together. How does that willingness come about? How far has, perhaps, sustained military training been effective in leading soldiers to perform acts they might never have envisaged in Civvy Street? Early in the last war, a regular army Colonel reminded me that the first duty of an officer towards his men was to teach them to obey orders without question; without that, discipline would collapse. That does not cover individually inspired, extraordinary, 'beyond the book', acts of bravery; or perhaps 'the book' includes the value of being able, in the right circumstances, to throw it away and act by individual impulse. Emerson went so far as to say that a great part of courage is the courage from having done this thing before; presumably that includes the effects of repetitive training.

Members of groups in war – batteries, regiments,

platoons, squadrons, ships' companies – are not individually recruited because they are known to be brave. That
expectation follows the recruitment and the training,
though some may meet it before they enrol, and some
may fail it when they are put to the test later. The aim is
to inculcate an inviolate group spirit so that no single one
of them will ever cut and run under fire. One officer, newly
appointed to our battery, did that. We kept quiet about it
because we would not have called it an act of cowardice.
Training had not worked and perhaps had been too hurried
at that time (1943). Certainly his legs took over beyond
anything he could do to control them.

Conversely, to stay put under, as in our case, attack from
the air and after thorough training may not be an act of
courage. The group sense of a small or large military unit
can well breed a kind of mutual courage, or what looks like
it.

Some 'acts of courage' seem to be blind, raw, unqualified.
Some will be called the utmost patriotism, and some of
those might be more accurately described as one-eyed
chauvinism. Behind some, though, there might lie a
considered decision, such as that this is the only possible
act before them, for the needs of battle or those of their
comrades. The language of citations can obscure a range
of possible impulses, from plain unthinking brute force to
deeply considered personal judgement; as no doubt
thoughtful officers and men know.

There are instances of men personally impelled to fight
to the utmost against a particular enemy; as Jews could feel
towards Nazis in the last war. A Jewish friend of mine after
some protective internment, since he had originally been a
refugee from Austria, once released enrolled in the
Commandos.

Perhaps a form of moral courage leading to death can be
found in the life of Frank Thompson, the elder brother of

the historian E. P. Thompson, who greatly cherished his memory. During the last war Frank chose to fight with Balkan forces against Fascist forces there. He and his group were captured and knew they would be executed. I understand that Frank Thompson died defiantly 'in the name of democracy'. That was clearly heroic, an expression of moral courage in the face of what he thought a barbarous philosophy. It might also be seen as self-deceiving obstinacy, overriding fear. Couldn't a loyal and convinced member of the Fascist forces have shown similar courage before death? One has to answer 'yes', to seek the principle behind each separate death, and make a judgement of that. If one's execution is accepted in defence of, for example, extreme racism, shouldn't that also be called 'moral courage' – in the face of an immoral belief. To me the death of Frank Thompson was an act of moral courage as were his life and acts on the way to that death. I cannot, though, see why that title should not be given to a Fascist who faces a similar death. Here my capacity for argument on moral principles gives up, obviously unable to go further.

Cowardice: Failures of Moral Courage

Cowardice and its inextricable ties to bravery are much commented upon, with the question of cowardice usually pre-eminent. An American proverb describes courage as 'fear that has said its prayers' and thus presumably girded itself. Walpole was nearer and deeper, in relating sober reflection to 'real courage'. 'Instantaneous' or 'cold' or 'two o'clock in the morning' courage, said Napoleon, was something he had rarely met.

G. B. Shaw was even more unromantic and thought cowardice as universal as seasickness; or, more accurately, he let a character in *Man and Superman* declare that opinion, meant to be startling and unattractive on first hearing. But when we relax our hidden wish to admire bravery, and add that seasickness can eventually be just about conquered by some so that they can return to duty, we may accept Shaw's ground-clearing frankness. It is partnered and given a fair coda by Rochester: 'For all men would be cowards if they durst.' In short, the fear of being labelled a coward can give courage to – a coward.

The most interesting of all such statements I have come across, because it points straight at what I think I am trying to define as true moral courage, is by C. S. Lewis. He argued that courage is not one of the virtues, but is: 'The form of every virtue at the testing point' (*The Screwtape Letters*).

I have seen only a few examples of what I would like to call unqualified moral courage; and more of its absence when called for. Some of the latter kind of instance may seem small but that does not invalidate them; they were real events and stay as firmly in the memory as do larger examples of cowardice and courage.

In North Africa I carried out a tricky mission over almost two weeks and several hundred miles, taking replacement guns and wagons from Algiers to a 25-pounder battery which had just been almost wiped out on a vulnerable bridge. I have told this at greater length elsewhere, but a brief version comes in well here, since the episode illustrates both cowardice and courage.

As we neared the end of the outward journey of almost a week, during which we had been regularly strafed by Stukas, dive-bombers, but had also enjoyed being members of a small group intent on a useful job, we had left the Atlas mountains and were on a large plain with little shelter. We had to have shelter for the night or would have been attacked, immobile, immediately on daylight. We found a

good clump of trees and I led the convoy to it. A major of
the Service Corps had already put his convoy there, but
there was room for more. He came up to me at the entry
point in a state of high emotion and ordered me to go
away. I refused; he 'pulled rank' and swore he would have
me court-martialled. I refused to yield to that. He persisted.
I imagine he may have thought our guns would have
glinted in the dawn light whereas his wagons were canvas-
hooded. Our guns were covered with camouflage netting
when bivouacked. The major went on in such an excited
state that it seemed like extreme cowardice; that he was,
in the usual army phrase, 'scared shitless'. He was prepared
to consign others to almost certain direct attack so as to
save his own (and of course his men's) skin. I think one can
call that moral cowardice. We moved in and found his men
unperturbed and friendly.

On our coming back from the mission my regimental
colonel was rather muted in his congratulations. The
adjutant, a very fair one at his job, told me that the
brigade major who had seen us off at Algiers docks – his
presence underlined the importance of the mission – had
informed my colonel that I should be formally repri-
manded if not court-martialled for arriving late at the
take-off point.

That was true; the lead truck driver, luckily not towing
a gun but carrying spares and food, was a young man fresh
from England and unused to the greasy and vergeless
Algerian roads. He put us in a very deep ditch. It took a
good few minutes to extricate the truck; even so, we arrived
at the starting point only five minutes late. I opened my
mouth to explain this to the major, who only shouted:
'*Shut up* – and get moving. You'll hear more of this.'

I told this to our colonel who of course accepted it
(and anyway the truck driver involved had driven me
back so could have testified), but said he wouldn't write

to the brigade major in explanation. He disliked what he liked to call 'fuss' and preferred the principle of 'water under the bridge'. I believe now that I should have written to the brigade major in my own defence. Still, I heard no more.

Later, I discovered that the colonel had originally told the adjutant to put me in for a Mention in Dispatches, for doing a good job. He had withdrawn the proposal after the brigade major had complained and did not reinstate it. I would call that, too, a failure of moral courage, however small, and perhaps aided by insensitivity; assisted also by the man's wish to keep his own nose clean with his superiors, even though that caused injustice to another below him.

—

A rather more complicated issue arose on a visit to the aboriginal territories of Northern Australia, in the late 1980s. We joined a group to see the remarkable cave paintings, so remarkable that they have special international status with UNESCO. They came within my portfolio during my time in Paris.

Apart from the two of us, almost all the passengers were middle-aged American couples. After about an hour the coach stopped and the driver waved at a single small cave with a few faint drawings on its walls. I was astonished, since the important cave to which the coach company promised a visit was about two hours from Darwin and had a substantial series of well-preserved paintings on several walls.

I went to the driver, indicated that I knew what had happened and asked him to drive on. He mulishly and silently ignored me. The other passengers were now back in their seats after looking at the feeble drawings. I told them we were not at all at our chosen destination and that I was sure of this because of my UNESCO connection. I asked them to join me in asking the driver to go further.

They sat stolidly in their seats, most with their heads down, and all silent.

Collective cowardice, reinforced by their shared national habits; 'do nothing so as to avoid a fuss.' How 'English' the Americans can be. I tried again, with the same result. I was both surprised and shocked. The driver engaged the gears and we went back to Darwin. No moral courage there.

Perhaps I should have made an even greater fuss on the spot. Had I threatened to report the driver's behaviour to his employers that would, as I learned later, have been useless. They were all in the scam. Still, I had enough of the English disinclination to cause a fuss to make me give up at that point on the bus; and that could be called a failure of moral courage on my part. I suppose it takes more important an instance of turpitude fully to turn on my sense of moral outrage. Even on the occasions when I do so act I am not always sure that I am drawing on a reserve of pure moral anger. Or is it, rather, an overwhelming feeling of personal outrage: that anyone could be so devious as they have just been. So, added to that is anger at 'being done'.

Tangentially, there can be, at least in the head, a strange reversal of the above reaction to attack or threat. It is the theme of a fascinating poem by the neglected writer A. S. J. Tessimond. The narrator is aware that his enemy is standing at his back, about to kill him. He simply accepts the situation, and pays for it. That seems to be neither a form of cowardice nor of courage; perhaps of extreme indifference to life and before death. Strange.

During the one free day before we left Darwin, I called again and again at the tour office; the manager was always out. I left a message and the name of our hotel; no response. Later I wrote to the tour firm's headquarters in, I think, Sydney. I also wrote to the domestic airline which shared in the promotion of the tour. No reply from any of them. I guess I had stumbled on a shared lying practice, so it had been felt better not to respond to any letters which showed they had been rumbled; lie low and hope the complainer was soon far away. Advance, Australia Fair!

Gulag, Holocaust and Other Group Challenges

Perhaps the widespread lack of reaction to the realities of the Gulag and the Holocaust may be seen as a form of collective moral – not so much cowardice, as deafness. What you have not apprehended you can hardly be guilty of cowardice towards, and so your moral reaction is inert.

For those who, unquestioning, carried out orders which sustained those horrors, moral choice had been subsumed under the second order morality of exactly acting on all instructions from above. But moral courage must mean refusing to do something which is against your own sense of morality because it does harm to others, even though your superiors order you to do so. Of course, to refuse may prove very costly, and few of us are heroes of that order.

So those two among the major events of the last century, the Gulag and the Holocaust, pose enormous challenges to our understanding of human wickedness and the difficulty of moral courage. That almost goes without saying more than was said much earlier, but not quite. The phenomenon deserves a few additional lines.

This must be a prime instance in human history of our ability to shrug off what might disturb us, especially since so much in modern communications is available to bring the horrors to our attention; if they and we so will. I am not implying that we should go about in public with banners round our necks, alerting all and sundry to such things. I am suggesting that here the human instinct to avoid the memory of horrible things, especially if they are by now in the recent past, makes common cause with much in modern mass communications, in whose interest it is not to recall such things too often. The mass media are by nature evasive towards the depressing. It is no doubt boring to repeat an old saw, but excusable here: those who ignore the past are doomed to repeat it. As I write, in some parts of Europe anti-Semitism has raised its ugly head again.

Further complicating elements remain to haunt us; that the Holocaust was committed by a so-called democratic nation which had become aberrant, though historically one of the most intellectually and artistically advanced of cultures. A few ideological fanatics, aided by several powerful elements in their society, persuaded or coerced the majority to accept their monstrous 'philosophy' and so took over absolute power. From that point all was possible and the road led to the Holocaust.

It would be difficult to assess the differences in evil between the Gulag and the Holocaust. The Gulag system was terrible, but in the beginning at least saw itself as one weapon towards a reformed society; that purpose faded as the terrible fanaticism of one man – or, perhaps fairer, two men – came to dominate. Not much of a justification, at any point. More, the Gulag did not emerge from an advanced democratic society, most of whose citizens were at least literate and to some extent able to read about and assess such a low level, such a brutish, activity.

Against both of those appalling activities a few heroic people stood up, spoke out and usually paid the price. They remind us that, though most of us do not respond to the need, moral courage can exist and hold fast until death.

If that were not so, then – especially to an agnostic – the future, the present-and-always condition of human kind, would be profoundly depressing. Evil would have won. Talk of the emergence of 'the civil society' would seem no more than jejune.

—

A more common, everyday, mean form of the failure to recognize the need for moral courage occurs when executives (and people beneath them) in many kinds of institution will 'swear black is white' in defence of a member or colleague against whom the evidence of misbehaviour is very strong. They usually find no dereliction there; or they argue that like institutions are similarly crooked and regularly put 'standing by your mate' before morality. Again, that secondary value, 'solidarity', or the milder-sounding but still secondary value, 'loyalty', take over here; as no doubt in other collectives.

A similar attitude intervenes when an individual in a position of some seniority refuses personally to act in a situation which requires at least some moral courage. This decline can be signalled by: 'I do take a more relaxed view of such things, you know.' 'Relaxed', like 'fuss', has become a weasel word. Or one hears: 'That's not really worth making a fuss about [a stand on] is it?' That from a boss to a subordinate is particularly corrosive.

Another and lower form of get-out or buck-passing occurs when a boss, faced with an action which unpleasantly requires moral courage, passes that decision with blank-eyed speed to a subordinate, excusing himself with: 'Not my baby, old boy'. I was lucky enough to meet the reverse of that on a couple of occasions during the war; more often matters went the other way.

There are instances, especially in international agencies,

where international civil servants are faced with severe personal problems. They may know, for instance, of their agency's Resolutions outlawing enforced female circumcision. They also know of Resolutions asserting the rights of individual cultures; and that their own country still practises enforced female circumcision, justifying itself by invoking the second Resolution and ignoring the first. What is a staff member who is a native of that country to do when this contradiction is discussed? He or she will know what is likely to happen to them, when their terms as international civil servants are finished and they return home, if they have not upheld their home country's 'cultural rights'. Usually their UNESCO superior finds a helpful manoeuvre – perhaps by giving them leave for a few days, during which the ambiguity will be discussed; and shelved for the time being.

Also at UNESCO I had a Soviet citizen (actually a Georgian, and incidentally a 'blues' enthusiast), in charge of one of the divisions I controlled. He knew when to keep silent if all departments and divisions were meeting round the table in my office, and was not urged to speak. As he left after one particularly difficult discussion, on Human Rights, he patted me on the shoulder and said: 'Thank you, my friend. You understand.' I am sure he was much happier after the Soviet Union broke up; but he died a few years ago.

I have been shuttling between the notion of the moral sense, and so of moral courage, as both a personal and a social/collective idea. To accept that last is to accept an enormous and difficult assumption. It was made when the Nuremberg Trials were held, a new invention and strongly defended by its proponents. Of course, many others objected to them in principle, seeing them as simply the vengeance of the victors purporting to be the expression of an outraged international moral sense. More than one English apophthegm ironically notes this habit, as one of the usual spoils of victory. The fighting being by then well over, few reflected on the Nuremberg Trials in either definition. A society which is just beginning to feel reasonably comfortable within itself does not easily query or rebuke itself.

Can the two elements – personal and collective responsibility – operate in the one society? In some matters, perhaps 'yes'. As in the decision of a society to outlaw capital punishment and racism, even if, as seemed the case here when these two laws were passed, a majority was not in favour of either change. No referendum was held on either. On BBC's Radio 4 recently a man phoned to ask on what grounds, since a majority favour capital punishment, could a democratically elected Parliament decide to abolish it; and also to outlaw racism. From his unqualified definition of a democracy he was right.

Nevertheless, this society's Parliament did pass both those laws and must have known that referenda might well have been against both. To go against public opinion was thought by Parliament to be in these matters within its rights. That was on a definition of democracy which held that the word does not mean a total following of the results of headcounts on all issues, no matter how troublesome or divisive some issues may be. Rather, it was assumed that the representatives of a democracy had the right to make decisions on certain issues according to the best thought-through opinions of those elected representatives, whether or not those might concur with majority opinion. And on these further safeguarding assumptions: that the representatives are elected for a fixed term, and subject to constant and well-nourished critical observation from all sorts of outside observers and institutions. No one could claim with total confidence that such provisos are always sufficient, but they go some way, and that way is always open to further and better democratic thinking.

Moral Courage in Action

After the above sizeable examples of weakness, can I produce at least one example of what seems like moral courage in action? I think so, in this instance an example both individual and collective, each intertwined; and military.

It concerns the 25-pounder artillery battery to which, as described earlier, I delivered replacement guns, wagons and – as it proved – drivers. On reaching the unit, we were surprised by the atmosphere of the place; strangely but not ominously quiet, busy but not bustling, intent on the often awful business but entirely unhistrionic. The battery commander was in a small tent, writing to the relatives of the many dead. The adjutant was preoccupied with the complex business of reforming the unit so that it was once again ready for action.

'I'll have to take all your drivers as well as the guns and wagons,' he said, without emphasis but as a matter of fact. 'I'll give you a receipt for them. Their kit will catch up with them.' That was very bad news for the men, but there was nothing to be done about it. 'I'd take you too', he added, 'but you aren't trained for handling this type of gun, so it will be better to get officer replacements from Base.'

The whole camp gave an example not only of the results of effective training but also, I think, of what can fairly be called collective moral courage. They had been through a nightmarish experience. They were going about their duties in a quiet, undemonstrative way; had buried their dead, seen to their wounded and heartened the survivors. They were putting in order their surviving equipment and taking over the replacements, doing all that was necessary so as to be again in good order for action, as soon as possible. They overrode the trauma. It went, again, beyond the results of good formal training to something more basically human. It had arrived at an understated, controlled, dignity and responsibility before disaster. It would be good to think that all units would in similar circumstances show such an elaborate set of admirable responses. Above all, that spirit seemed to flow quietly but firmly down from the CO and adjutant to all ranks; as is right.

Love and Charity

Moral courage, it is plain, for an atheist or agnostic as for a Christian, must be based on, at bottom drawn from, our attitude toward others; and that is based on the willingness and ability to reduce our own self-love. What is that desirable attitude to be called? A Christian will reply unhesitatingly: 'Oh, Love, Love for one another, universal Love.'

Here I have found myself in doubt, doubt precisely about the all-embracing application of the demand for Love. Linked with and arising from that, as one of my own most powerful impulses, seems to be what I have come round to calling not 'Love' but, rather, 'Charity'. This is not to say that I lack Love so far as I am able to recognize it, but rather that in relations with those not connected with me by family ties or close friendship, but who ask for understanding from me, I call upon the impulse of charity; which is not necessarily an easily expressed attitude or act. Love requires something more of a relationship. 'Love thy neighbour' I know as a Christian admonition; I find it verges on the over-undiscriminating, and prefer: 'Show charity to all.' That may indicate in me a fundamental fear of opening myself to all but a known few. I am not convinced of that. Or it may be Northern emotional inhibition. Or a sound distinction.

I could, without the benefits of religion, try to give a utilitarian justification for a belief in the overriding power of Love (exercise it and trust that that will be reciprocated.

'Do unto others as you would be done by.'). But that would not fit, since many other less attractive attitudes – to do with keeping an eye on all sorts of debts owed, from physical to moral, and repayments due from others – could be brought within that kind of contract. I believe, without religious support, that charity should be both one – and many – sided, offered even if not returned. So, again without religion – though the idea itself may have been instilled by the early insistence that we are all 'Children of God' – I am left saying rather mutedly but not nervously, that without charity our lives would be as nothing; thus doing something to resist a judgemental though not necessarily a judging attitude.

Chapter 7

Words and Writing

I am convinced more and more and day by day that fine writing is, next to fine doing, the top thing in the world.

(Keats, Letter to J. H. Reynolds, 24 August 1819)

Not a Natural

Not long ago I was rereading with amusement and admiration, especially for his wit and narrative skill, one of Kingsley Amis's novels. After a few moments I recognized for the first time that an important reason for my enjoying his work is the apparent easiness of his style, the natural sense of rhythm, of just where to drop an adverb or close a sentence; a sort of rightness about his prose, so that you felt he could hardly produce a clumsy sentence. The ability was in his being; he was a 'born pro'.

In short, I learned this unexpectedly, suddenly and directly; not from one of the usual classical models, but from someone who was a few years younger than I, and whose reputation will no doubt change over the years.

—

Since I have spent much of my spare time over sixty years in writing, I had better say at the start – though some will also dismiss this, at the start too, as false modesty – two things: I do not think that as compared with Kingsley Amis I have a born writer's talent, nor feel I belong to the 'English Literary Happy Family', whose members I have seen at occasional gatherings, greeting one another with familial warmth. Yet I belong to the Society of Authors, the Royal Society of Literature and PEN.

Yet still I go on writing; without quite knowing why. It would be altogether too grand to label this the response to a 'call'. A sense of duty? Not quite. A sense of need (in me)? That is nearer, but self-evident; otherwise, I wouldn't be writing these particular lines. An unexplained urge, perhaps, whose results one can discuss better than its origins.

At any rate, I have been over all those years, and remain, a bit of a loner; as some earlier pages also bore out. Sometimes, I wonder what influence, if any, the sense of being part of a known group, affects some writers. Iris Murdoch mingled happily; I do not think this affected her writing; though her subjects, yes. She did often write about intellectual groups, but that fact did not often decide either approach or style.

Perhaps we have to look at a more commercial type of writer to find group attitudes and styles. Here we come most notably upon the genre novels, the Aga Sagas, chick lit and the rest. I was once given a lesson in differences; between people such as myself who start, to put the matter extremely simply, by thinking they may have something to say and hope that will be thought interesting by some readers; and reader-directed writers in a commercial sense.

The Commercial Urge

I was once invited to speak to a Writers' Group. Apart from their tutor (it was a class organized by the Local Educational Authority), only women were present. It was obvious soon after the start that most were disappointed. I might have been a Mongolian herdsman describing the ancient type of weaving with which he filled the long hours watching his goats. To them, I was rather painfully airy-fairy, in particular by asking them what drove them to choose this subject rather than that. They knew, without self-questioning or questioning from outsiders. No special problem about getting in touch there; only the need to follow existing tastes by latching on to the right magazines.

I realized these things only when questioning began after my introduction. At that point one bolder than the others said: 'I know whom I write for – the readers of women's magazines. I don't look inside myself. Those readers decide my subjects for me. I thought you might have had some advice to give us about that, but you haven't done so.' Very articulate. Most of the others nodded. Some others outside would have nodded too, including some popular novelists, who spin variations on well-known themes and attitudes and hope for a large advance against an expected best-seller and perhaps even the sale of film rights.

Certain of these authors may have talent, but it will probably have been confined by their own limiting of their aims. They may not be aware of this and neither may their readers. A very few may later, like chickens from their shells, break out by instinct and then be surprised by what they have done. Others will succeed in the usual ways and be rewarded for that.

Outsiders of Different Kinds

First, then, may come the urge to write, wherever you are and whether you are gifted. I stress the latter because, although you may not regard yourself as greatly gifted, you will meet on the way some who clearly are not; but who go on hopefully writing. The latter-day sons and daughters of Casaubon. They may or may not use big words to justify what they are about; they are unlikely to speak of fame, even less of money, or of a place in posterity. They are even less likely to claim to being 'in the truth', though I have met one who trembled on the edge of that declaration. Others, I think, should be encouraged if there seem to be any grounds for doing so; but not given false hopes. It perhaps goes without saying that much writing of this kind is autobiographical.

Even the most aspiring of would-be writers may sooner or later, and whether or not they are willing to take them, come upon hints as to whether they 'have a future'. That need not happen, but I have the impression that few give up and most go on having 'something in hand' and probably leave bulky manuscripts when they die. Often they ask that these be forwarded to a writer they feel will be sympathetic. I have been led to write briefly about this small army because they receive little attention; and because they should be respected. They have hold of an important truth: words, writing, matter.

Word-deaf?

Now for a different sort of person. It is quite hard for anyone who loves literature, whether predominantly as a writer or reader, to recognize that, outside, are people devoid of any such wish, who would think it odd to write

106

for any except a functional purpose and so in a functional manner. (Purely incidentally, the writing of most instructions to non-specialists prepared by specialists could do with a prior glance from a 'real' writer – a poet, say.) Those people I now have in mind and whom I first met, oddly enough, in adult literature classes, are not responsive to any works of literature. Introduce them to some of the finest, the most moving, poems of Wordsworth or Tennyson or half a dozen others and they will honestly and unaggressively tell you that they feel nothing at all. They are, as it were, word-deaf. It would be easy to dismiss them as insensitive, lacking imagination. Are composers and fine instrumentalists lacking in imagination? Or visual artists? Mathematicians are likely to speak of a solution as 'elegant', which can suggest imagination at work.

Here the problem intensfies. We justly say that literature can increase our insights into and understanding of 'the human condition'. Literature's words for all shades of human experience offer that, but we cannot claim that that is the only way to feed the budding imagination. But literature is a superb gateway. Are those who seemed deaf to the power and beauty of poetry to be assumed to be deaf to Jane Austen? I know from my adult students that that is not so. It would seem that our imaginations and our reason cooperate to read different kinds of literature differently; and that some have dead imaginative keys but lively ratiocinative ones.

Nowadays, depending on their self-confidence cooperating with their pride as eminent public figures, some who are apparently word-deaf will confidently deny any claims for what others call great literature. Like the 'celebrities' themselves, that attitude is a product of contemporary levelling.

Recently, two such 'Television Personalities', one an expert on motor cars, the other a mathematician, firmly asserted not that they were deaf to Shakespeare but that there was nothing of interest in his work. 'I don't see it, so it doesn't exist' – even though over six centuries and all over the world, countless millions of the literate have hailed Shakespeare's power over their minds and hearts. That might have induced a little modest hesitation. But that is not today's way. On that as on anything else, 'my opinion is as good as anyone else's' dominates. Off-the-cuff opinion triumphs over informed judgement. Not that the above two apply that kind of thinking to motor cars or maths. A similarly silly dispute was fomented by the mass media over the merits or failings of Joyce's *Ulysses*, initiated by a minor-celebrity writer who saw no merit there.

Words Themselves

A word from a scientist may come in well here. A. N. Whitehead wrote, rather grandly but literary people can hardly object, that: 'The canons of art are merely the expression in specialized form of the requisites for depth of experience.' One can imagine some of Whitehead's scientific colleagues simply rejecting that, and others perhaps being made to think again. But it would be better if 'merely' were replaced by 'uniquely'.

So for me, as I expect for many like me, everything started with words individual or grouped. I soon heard about, read and took on board words with moral weight, judging words: 'straightforward–decent–comely–charity–tolerance–tenderness–respectable–companionable–demotic.' And on the other hand: 'Trivial–small-minded–smoothie chops–smarty-pants–snide–doing down'. It should be fairly easy to put together a rough sketch of an author's character from the use of those two groups; obviously.

Oddly, single words, not necessarily abstractions, can lead to complex thoughts. In *Faust*, Goethe noted that sometimes, when thought was stuck, a single word could pop up and release it. That recognizes the natural interplay between the power of meaning and the force of suggestion. Near, but not quite on that point, Auden realized that a word accidentally introduced into a poem – perhaps by a typesetting error – may be more felicitous, more right, than the original. In *Letters from Iceland* he had written, 'And the poets have names for the sea.' A typesetting error produced: 'And the ports have names for the sea', which he accepted happily, presumably as more evocative of the weighty, often sad, always complex, relations between port and sea, and less turned in towards the poet than his original.

From such instances it is clear, if it was not before, that words are more complexly connected to meaning than as simple indicators, pointers, but are part of the very process of thought and imagination. They have different natural weights, sometimes light, sometimes heavy. They can 'programme' us, push us towards some good acts in writing or in life, or to some we may come to regret.

Related to the single words are brief sentences or small incidents which stick in the mind because they are, to alter the angle, eye- or ear- or nose-catching. This was the discovery by a couple who had let their flat for a year to some students at the Royal College of Music; middle-class young women. On the owners' return they found, among other depredations, that the lavatory bowl was, all over and heavily, so caked in shit that industrial cleaners had to be called in. Nothing else in their casual careless occupation was so telling: Music, Youth, Class and Daily Life; what a mixture.

A horrific example, which too will not go away, records something of a pocket tragedy. A social worker lived for a time in a semi-detached house on an Oxford council estate.

One evening she heard, through the thin walls, a father pushing a daughter upstairs. She resisted with: 'Eh, Dad, 'ave our Mavis. You 'ad me yesterday.'

Years ago, a friend heard me tell a story about elderly gentlemen paying guardsmen in Hyde Park to pee into their trouser pockets. He had heard it before but noticed a slight addition by me. I had said: '*left* trouser pocket'. A curious urge for unnecessary precision, but it also increases the life of the passage. As in *Great Expectations*, where Mr Pumblechook is robbed and assaulted. They didn't muzzle him or simply 'stuff his mouth'. They: 'stuffed his mouth *with flowering annuals*'. Wonderful; and probably where I first noticed the device. It's the mad superfluous precision that does it.

Images and Incidents

The love of images, if given scope in public life, can lead to trouble. They may be colourful, clear, brief and apt; but they can be turned against you. As I sometimes forget. I once had, and without the usual briefing, to announce the ending of the Arts Council's grant to a training company for young actors. Its record had become very poor, as Council officers and advisers had more than once said, in-house but rarely in public. The Council is – or was – congenitally soft-hearted. But finally it had to decide to tell the company that its grant was seriously at risk.

The company mounted a vigorous and none-too-scrupulous defence. The issue was raised at a Press Conference at which, in the absence of the Chairman, I spoke for the Council. It became clear that members of the Press there did not know that the company had been warned more than once that they would need to do better if they were to retain their grant. I made that plain.

Nevertheless, a journalist asked why the grant was to be cut off without warning, 'peremptorily'. I told him, as should have been clear from our report circulated in advance and from what I had just said, that 'peremptorily' was not the right word, that there had been ample advice and warnings.

As the meeting ended, the journalist, anxious for a soundbite all to himself, caught me as I reached the door and asked: 'Why couldn't you have given them another chance? Wouldn't that have been more *democratic*?' As if he really cared for anything except a striking headline. He got that. 'Art' and 'Democracy' can make uneasy bedfellows, especially when in capitals and inverted commas.

I allowed myself to be irritated, and my weakness for colourful imagery took over. I replied that there could be too many stays of execution for the health of any profession. That was all the journalist needed to produce that evening an inflammatory, loaded headline on my and the Council's 'hangman's methods'. On the following morning a group picketed the Council's offices on Piccadilly, carrying banners some of which were labelled: 'Hang Hoggart high.' Overcolourful metaphors can return to haunt you.

I did not learn that lesson quickly enough. In a later literary judging committee I thought that one book, though a close contender, was not the best. An image, which I have by now forgotten, floated into my mind to illustrate its weaknesses as I saw them. A literary agent was an 'observer' on the committee. I learned later that he was a congenital gossip. He duly told the author concerned, who understandably had had good hopes that he would win, about my image. The book did not win. I do not think my image was decisive, but the author may probably still bear me a grudge.

—

The Process of Writing

My own occasional uncertainty affects the actual process of writing, so that I have rarely been able effectively to establish a daily pattern of work, a control for the ups and downs. I think sometimes, with a slightly jealous awe, of those – Trollope is a superb example – who can sit down at a set time each day, for a set number of hours and produce a substantial amount of at least adequate prose.

Several good writers argue that that kind of discipline is essential for a serious professional. I can occasionally go so far as to sit down, feeling dumpy and fit only for inscribing the alphabet two or three times. Usually, that feeling slowly lifts. It is as though a faucet, gradually at first, has been released; or a tree trunk tapped for its perhaps niggardly juice. From then on, I can probably put in an hour or two of, in my terms, reasonable writing; or even find something of a flow. That feeling is part sensuous, due to being physically comfortable. Added to that is the feeling that, if I pass more than about a month without having a book 'on the go', I begin to feel like a dog with no tail; or rudderless, lost, deserted – tongueless.

As to style, my debts to Butler and Orwell arose from the search for a clear unembroidered manner. I am now more often smelling Henry James's style as though at a peculiarly rich and complex bloom. Simplicity for clarity and cleanliness of purpose can have an honest athleticism. Naturally, a rich tapestry can carry greater complexities, qualifications, windings in, out and around. Good prose is not always like a window-pane.

For Whom?

At the back of my mind, if I find myself led towards thinking of possible readers, I remember that Conrad, in one of his meatily chewed-over Prefaces, has his narrator Marlow say that his aim is to make his hearers *see*; and adds that his hearers are in this helped because they can see him, the narrator, whom they know. They will be helped by seeing double: the characters and their situations in the novel, and the narrator who is the prism through which they see those people and happenings. I can see the inadequacy of an attempt to apply Conrad's image entirely to the role of an autobiographer, but there is some similarity. The autobiographer wants you to believe in the tale he tells; and also hopes that his own personality will validate it; a matter of achieved trust.

Chekhov takes all this much further: 'It is the writer's business not to accuse and not to prosecute, but to champion the guilty once they are condemned and suffer punishment.' That goes to the ultimate, beyond the relative simplicities of 'trying to understand' and, more, of judging without being judgemental. There is no privileged utterance; only a humane hope, through the way the words work.

That – 'the way the words work' – is the most important element. As often, Nietzsche got the point: 'To improve one's style is to improve one's thought and nothing else.' What else could one hope for? Many of us think the process works in the opposite way.

From Gossip to Anecdote – and On

Apparently, I cannot write a novel, much as I would like to. I love anecdotes; not gossip, from which anecdotes ought to be ring-fenced. Anecdotes are the granular fertilizers to the soil of many novels, uniquely clarifying and exposing. In his Preface to *Nostromo* Conrad recalls how 'a vagrant anecdote' set him off on that novel.

Gossip is made up of cocktail snacks with no body and a nasty aftertaste. They can never become the substantial part of a meal, which sustains. It says 'Ooh, ah!', but doesn't open our eyes or mind, and can't be lingered over. Anecdotes can shimmer in the memory.

Gossip, until you turn against it, can be horribly engaging. It has one foot in the mud. Its upright sister, anecdote, has broken clear and invites you to reflect on human nature. Both are connected with the novel, in that they enjoy 'telling the tale' and love images. Gossips and anecdotalists thrive on metaphor; it is the sauce with which their dishes are spiced. At bottom, gossip is envious and malicious, pleased to see anyone brought down, especially those who have sought to move upward. Even its praise is almost always adulterated, a form of self-congratulation for being willing to give modest praise to others. Which is why gossips, though avidly listened to, are at bottom shunned, hated. Gossip can help knit a group of streets together, in fascination with the story and dislike of the teller. The streets recognize them 'for what they are', greedily listen to them at first or second or third hand; and dislike them.

Unfortunately, as we grow older we can find anecdotes also an easy way of evading sustained thought about the meaning of relationships. Even so, anecdotes have their own rules which gossip lacks: accuracy, relevance, aptness, implication and weight. It is plain that I have come to dislike gossip whilst continuing to enjoy anecdote – and all the more to recognize that its true, final, bedded home is the novel.

At this point I wonder yet again why, since I admire novels so much, I have firmly decided that writing novels is not for me. Perhaps a very few elements in my writing would be at home in the novel. I doubt, for instance, whether any competent handling of relationships or the intricacies of a social panorama over time would be revealed.

Ah, the novel; the workhorse of literary forms, the carpet-bag touched with magic, Lawrence's 'one bright book of life'. It must be marvellous to feel ready and willing to take that on and for several hundred pages; such grindingly hard work; and to try to bring it off. However did Tolstoy manage to hold all that together for fifteen hundred pages? There must have been depressions on the way. My own brief attempts kept dragging me back to the individual eye; warm breath on the back of the reader's neck. A related error, in the novel proper, is what Lawrence called: 'putting your thumb in the scales'. I once detected what seemed a clear instance of that and mentioned it to the author. He was neither convinced nor amused. The habit is, naturally, endemic in autobiography; there, the rules can seem, but not be, less rigid.

I realize why Forster regretted that the novel had to tell a story – that piece of string the author had to keep tight hold of, that 'what happens next' element. The interest in anecdotes then becomes clearer; they are useful knots on the string. It is interesting that Henry James, who wove so many intricacies into the carpet of his novels, also respected the importance of that ball of string and kept good hold of it.

The drama? Years ago, a BBC producer urged me to write a play. So I began; and gave up after Act 1, Scene 1. The reasons were clear and simple. My poor characters, insofar as they existed at all, were endless talkers, of monologues, though now and again they let others have a go. Worse, they did not move. I could not see them in three-dimensional space in which they came and went, had their exits and entrances. They talked all the time, quietly or heatedly, and stayed tied to the one spot. No one came in to introduce a new element. No one left, if only to answer a call of nature. Not even a loo-chain was pulled off stage, to suggest other humans outside. All the characters stayed, talking perhaps but also mutely begging for release, to be taken out of the selfish world of the single authorial voice, and to be granted an instance of dramatic surprise.

—

So: back to autobiography. About which, one has at this point to say, that it is almost always to some extent a form of preoccupying self-love, of vanity – in thinking your life is worth all that attention, even if only as an example. It is hard work, not as hard as writing a novel, but each element, incident, observation should go through a fine sieve. You know that that sieving cannot be altogether successful – self-love is tenacious – but you have to try in hope; and put up with the strain on the sense of honesty. Self-justification is always present, so self-censorship has also to be on duty; so long as self-love allows. As to modestly recognizing one's own virtues; they should not be made explicit. Best to let them emerge obliquely, as reverse reflections, from among much else; insofar as there are any to emerge. Autobiography is partly self-absorbed; it is just as much an escape from self.

It is in fact a somewhat complex fate, to try to be an autobiographer. There is no escape from that mill, from that bootstrap-lifting effort. Of course, some do better than others. Herbert Read and Edwin Muir are good examples of a grave search for integrity. But what about Henry Adams? He employs all sorts of artifices; blatantly, one might say. For me, they work. The personality emerges, nearly warts and all. Which goes to prove that the prescriptions suggested above are, like all prescriptions, only partially true.

So in old age, and in a phrase which has become recurrent here, we 'go on going on'; in some ways trying to fend off the inevitable, aiming to get down to some writing which might last at least for a few years. To use another favourite image: sometimes you feel like a screwed-up tea bag from which you hope to squeeze a last cupful. And sometimes feeling rather more hopeful than that.

—

I do not wish to sit in the garden looking at the flowers or listening to the birds. I am neither a Joiner of Societies nor a Hobbies man. In spite of what I said much earlier about why I feel that I must write, when I dismissed rather grand words such as a 'calling', I do feel 'recruited' and hope to die obeying the modern equivalent of 'with my boots on' – with my fingers on the keyboard.

Umberto Eco has a neat romantic phrase for one's wish at this point; that one may hope to have left 'a message in the bottle', one which to you seems worth bottling.

Chapter 8

Memory

Largely Personal

Throughout these pages there have had to be references to the power of memory. Now, towards the end, it seems right to gather them together, add to them, and perhaps manage to make more general sense of the ways memory works.

To begin with a large generalization: memory is an enormous octopus, constantly twining and untwining multiple limbs which nevertheless are all connected to a huge central carcass.

By now, one finds that various forms of memory-slippage go on developing. Long-term memory, which used to be taken for granted, now shows large blank spaces. You have always assumed that everything you have ever experienced is somewhere, and recoverable. You do not have, and do not want, a form of Delete Button. But neither do you have a Recycling Bin from which items which have accidentally been deleted can be recovered. But very little is accidentally lost.

You feel embarrassed and ashamed when an acquaintance reminds you that a good few years ago you had lunch with her father, now dead. She had not been present

119

but gives precise details of place, and of some of the conversation. Clearly, it had been, for her father, a very interesting occasion, For you, nothing she says produces a single beam of light from which the occasion can be recovered.

Most frequent and embarrassing: more and more you forget names from both long ago and recently. Some still come back after a few moments; others seem firmly lost. This makes you feel foolish in company and critical towards yourself.

Short-term memory begins to fail also, like images removed too quickly from a portable screen by an unseen hand. Some memories should, one feels, be built into the very repetitive pattern of our days, but we still muddle them: 'If we are preparing to shop this morning it must be Tuesday. Or Friday? But on Friday mornings we usually feel a slight lift at the approach of the weekend. No lift. So it's probably Tuesday.' But why should there still be a bit of a lift on Fridays? They no longer mark the end of the working week. Yet, as I noted much earlier, weekends do still feel different. It is easy to see what marks the weekends for the religious. For us, too, they are still more relaxed, off the hook, open-ended, a time for doing something out of the ordinary – if we can think of a 'something' like that. That blank cheque is now rarely cashed. Except when our children or their children call.

Long- and short-term memories, or the failure of them, constantly interact in unexpected ways. You remember from long ago a kindness, or an unpleasantness, but forget the name of someone who talked interestingly only a few days ago. It seems easy to explain that. Long-term memory can retain treats for us and even minor as well as major injuries. Meanwhile, we forget that we have left a bucket in the kitchen sink filling with water; or that the garage still has its keys in the lock. Those last two – the bucket and the garage – should really be seen as belonging to another category, of things which have not belonged even in the container for short-term memories. They are held in a special space at the very front of the mind, ready as needed, and then deleted, till next time. That automatic process has not been wholly retained. Some of such small, routine, repetitive activities have now no home. Yet some 'front of mind' thoughts have increased; such as worries when the children and their families have gone abroad on holiday; that bit of the mind has lost some of its bounce. They belong not to the long or short term but in an Instant Memory box.

A very few of the trammelling habits you have had since childhood still hold their ground. Those are the exceptionally long-term, or the without-term.

Places are easier. They fill the pictorial memory like a restroom for the aged with scenes all round the walls. The Lakes and their mountains as first seen from a bicycle as you breast the last hill before Keswick; the Cotswolds on our honeymoon, quiet as not before or since; the homely Dorset coast with the family; and so on and so on – all giving that sense of well-and-long-lived-in time and space which this small island exudes.

I could enumerate places abroad at boring length, especially those opened to us by UNESCO. Just one entry: of all the ancient sites we saw across the whole world, Machu Picchu is pre-eminent, after several centuries dug out of an ancient forest, the lost town of a lost civilization, among what we used to call 'ageless' landscapes. That demands that we try to reassess our own space and time – after we have captured the scene with our digital cameras.

Yet, as is evident by now, most deep-rooted of all are the Yorkshire Dales; from adolescence on. Hardly a town, small villages with bowed stone bridges, farmsteads with pots of tea for a few pence in refurbished barns, pebbly fast-running rivers, misty hills, narrow winding roads, handmade stone walls, wide air, springy, thyme-laden grass, curlews and plovers, long 'hikes' and cycle rides. All that will die for us but not with us. Youth is not, after all, 'wasted on the young'. Many from those of two generations after us are treading those acres as I write, exchanging the statutory "Ow dos?' as they pass.

—

Evidently, for most of us, the exercises of memory are dominant as gateways to ourselves, to what we have been and are, the older we become. Eighty or round about that figure is, in our experience, the period when you first recognize this force. Much is lost, long or short, important or trivial, as you will often be reminded by others; or, slightly later in most instances, by your own hidden back-memory checking system. Yet memory has its compensations; it looks backwards and shuttles endlessly. It keeps us in touch well beyond the power of photographs or cherished objects. It is alive, the most active element of old age, a metaphorical lifeline.

The actual process of memory, the way it seems to work, is always fascinating and often distressing. It constantly changes tack so that one thing follows another without logical connection, but with an emotional or even imaginative link. Its orders of importance are not ours, or are ours well below the conscious surface of likes and dislikes, and of accepted significances.

Its rules are its own. So I remember well the faces of fellow officers from sixty years ago, but not all their names. I remember even more sharply than their faces their characters as I thought of them, based on willingness to share work, likely reaction in a crisis and general companionableness. I remember as a group, an admirable body of men, who drove the huge wagons which towed the guns.

Most of them in peacetime steered HGVs (Heavy Goods Vehicles) up and down the roads of Britain. They had a fine fellowship of their own and it carried through to their war service and affected us all, for the good.

The faces, names and characters of some academic colleagues from forty years ago are less clear. It would be easy entirely to explain that difference by recalling that in the army we lived on top of each other day by day for several years, but that does not seem sufficient. Our ages at that time would be another factor, plus the moments of great challenge; all composing the feeling that we were living exceptionally, out of time.

Memory can be wilful and apparently inconsequential. Why do I remember at least once a month a fragment of conversation fifty years ago, with a man (we were shaving side by side in a university hostel) in which he said that 'once shaved is half-shaved'. Not very important advice, but – a trigger a day, or every few days. Perhaps its air of an old saw made it stick, but I could well do without it.

Memory also startles because it can recall events which shocked us beyond what we were expecting. I said earlier that I am deeply upset to see anyone crying in public; that is surely not exceptional? But much the strongest reaction was to see a middle-aged man who had just heard that his sister had died. He collapsed weeping on a seat. Would the response to a middle-aged woman who had had such news been similar? Yes, would seem to be the answer. My memory has decided otherwise. I have seen a woman cry in public and been shocked. I remember much more forcefully the sight of the middle-aged man described above. Apparently somewhere in my mind I find the sight of a man crying more distressing, more against nature, than the sight of a woman similarly affected.

I now see that my own memories are on the whole – well, often – emotionally, historically and intellectually structured; by the initial family break-up, marriage and children, and writing. Almost all else hangs around those.

Hurts, even if to an outsider inconsiderable, can last longer than they are worth. My brother was best man at my wedding; that seems the obvious familial gesture. At his, later, wedding the best man was his closest friend, and I was a little miffed. That gradually faded, as I appreciated better the critical place of a best friend outside the very large family which he had been sent to when we were orphaned. That was not due to unkindnesses in his new home, but to the development of intellectual and other new interests in him.

At this point I recall the role of the family historian or memory-keeper; many, perhaps most, families have one. In my experience, those are not the most cunningly selective but rather the most tenaciously collective. They seem to want to remember all and only occasionally judge between elements or people; in particular when one commits some quite unusual act, as in 'going off the rails', or metaphorically and perhaps actually 'going to the dogs'. Collective family memory only sells the family down river if that has an event or events too obvious to bury; and those are likely to be known abroad anyway.

But for most of us memories tend to be all mixed, good and bad, important or trivial. I can recall only one person who seemed likely to have nothing but good memories. If anyone had ever done him wrong he seemed to have forgotten; he had what appeared to be a perfectly, always equable, marriage and children to match. He seemed to have what looked like a two-dimensional life revolving round home and occupation; he worked in wrought iron, making garden gates, door knockers and the like. His job fitted his character. He was a 'very nice' man, but a little dull.

General Observations on Memories in Us All

On the whole, we do not control memories; they *control* us, without our full knowledge. So sometimes we remember things we think little of, but which later earn their passage by revealing their importance. We may wish them all to be pleasant but discover that we remember most often and keenly those which went most deeply into the heart, more deeply than we at the time realized, and stayed there, whether happy or sad. Few memories are unalloyed and our memory knows better than we do which will most count in the long run.

Memories work *underground*. As they meet and discover their connections they can clear our thoughts; not always pleasantly.

Matthew Arnold said we have to *forget* some memories because we could not live easily with them. Was he arguing that though it can be very difficult to erase memories, we have to try to will that; and may eventually succeed. Memories can be powerful reminders; of some things rather than others.

Memories can gradually become *false*, eroded, worn out, misleading. After a while two person's accounts of the same incident and its implications will differ widely and each will be convinced that theirs is the 'right' description; much is at at stake for each of them.

Memory's orders of importance are not necessarily ours. But for important reasons those *orders* can eventually seem more accurate to us than our own first claims. Does that mean that we have reached a more important truth? Or only one more liveable with?

Sometimes we think we have somehow *removed* a memory; but it is always lurking in the background and will 'out', especially if a much later link pops up and prompts it again.

A person very strong mentally but not necessarily a more admirable person may to some extent *learn to control* memory and so save a lot of time. But that impression of power may well be mistaken. Memory itself is not an act of the intelligence. It is the enemy of intellect and, even more, of imagination; its world is that of the personal emotions.

Can we, by an act of will, from the start train ourselves to remember something of great importance to us? Only if we *write* it down, and that is an evasion though acceptable. It will usually escape from the mind itself.

'Old men forget', but they will not forget Agincourt, said Henry V. Most of us have no such *compelling* memory; except from wartime. I have one such, and see myself as clearly as on the day itself, being carried on a broken door to the Regimental Medical Centre, before the morphine took over.

Of the five *senses*, which best recalls memory? That is likely to differ from person to person. For me, taste is important, but smell is dominant. Yet emotion as a memory inducer does not depend on any of the senses. It operates alone.

What is the relationship between memory and *nostalgia*? Nostalgia is sticky memory, unable to let memory stand free; emotion has overflowed.

Sometimes memory becomes very *moral*; or moralistic. I do not understand how this works. Perhaps it is an escape from the intellect, or from considered thought; it is moving on to the relevant emotions.

The memory has a powerful hold on our capacity for *regret*. Recall only the many poems which connect the two. And the timeless aphorisms which recognize the need to escape from regrets, such as that which tells us it is no use closing the stable door after the horse has gone or, more homely, that it is no use crying over spilt milk. Worst of all, regret over things not done when chance appeared – especially good things; and regrettable things done which cannot now be undone. We now regret both as failings. The doors to both kinds of recompense closed long ago.

Since memory is now, in old age, even more exercised than it has formerly been, we are prompted to look backward across the whole panorama and ask ourselves how much we have learned all along the way; about ourselves and our relations with others; and about society. A brief honest answer would be: 'Something was learned, yes, and I have acknowledged that as we went along. But not as much as I had hoped.'

Faced daily with memories good, bad and indifferent, would I like to live them all again? Or a chosen few? Yes, to the chosen few. But also I would want still to be able to write about them, to try to make better sense of them. Writing helps us to cope, for some memories do not help there, but will not go away. There can be no consolation in them, nothing to nourish, and the present can feel then as though it is not to be long borne. But those are exceptional dips. On the whole, memory is more a friend than a foe. Or so, at present, I think.

Now we link again with Chapter 1; on old age, before we thought more directly of death; as we do now.

Epilogue

Among Thoughts of Death

Death must be distinguished from dying, with which it is often confused.

(Sydney Smith in. H. Pearson,
The Smith of Smiths, Ch. II, p. 271)

Preliminary Muddles

To quote from T. S. Eliot's *The Waste Land*. Looking at the London crowds, the poet found himself surprised that 'death had undone so many.' I am similarly surprised that so few seem to have written about the approach of death.

Sydney Smith's contrast is puzzling, and I am not yet sure that I fully understand it. In one obvious sense we all and all the time separate death from dying; or, perhaps more obviously, dying from death, the usual natural succession. 'Usual' rather than 'inevitable' because we do not all have that experience. Some of us die without warning to ourselves or others; from violence, a stroke, an accident or heart attack. No 'dying' there, just death. Dying can be slow, long, and for any attendant observers may be a poignant, memory-filled process; worse than death itself.

Death, the moment of death, is by definition usually sudden and, so far as we know, blank to the sufferer. A switching off of the light. Sydney Smith seems to be pointing to something more important, even momentous. He may even be implying that the nature of dying, as a prolonged or sad or sometimes composed matter, may be to some extent decided for each of us by character, whereas death is a final emptiness for us all.

Nor does that seem quite right. It is possible to argue – it is obvious – that our process of dying begins the moment we are born. No deep suggestion there, and not likely to be what Sydney Smith meant. 'He is dying, so try to see him before he goes' is common advice, and suggests that 'dying' is often a process in the immediate ante-room. It is still not obvious that death is, as Sydney Smith claimed, often confused with dying.

We are getting nowhere. What Sydney Smith meant may become clearer as we go along here, but I am not at all sure of that. To some the statement may seem at once and obviously full of meaning.

Time; and Courtesies

We may more directly start, however, with a picture of death itself, with one of the dead. A television documentary film showed the inside of a municipal mortuary. The naked body of an extremely fat man lay on a slab, being made ready for burial or cremation, and needing to be moved in various ways. The staff throughout referred to the body as: 'This gentleman', as in: 'Please could you help me lift this gentleman, Tom?.' That gave the corpse dignity. Did the staff speak in that way because they were being filmed? That is possible. Or it could have been their normal procedure, meant not to rob the dead of all respect. To an

130

onlooker it was touching. Similarly, when I was in hospital for a few days, a nurse bringing my breakfast said: 'I'm sorry to have to tell you that the gentleman in the next bed [a cancer patient] died in the night.'

For many of us the idea of death seems to occur at intervals; from, say, our mid-forties; and earlier if we have children, when responsibility increases apprehension. In extreme old age, at which in my late-eighties I must be presumed to have arrived, it can be habitual to think not only of the progress of ageing but of dying and death, that last probably not far off. 'I lay me down to sleep; and may not awake.' This need not necessarily be obsessive or depressive. Just as often, on some days quite often, one finds oneself remembering with pleasure, rather suddenly and unexpectedly, large and small things. It may be assumed that there is not much time left, so let them be filled with memories of what was good in what went before; and have some good newer experiences – if you can manage that effort. Some days you will not be able to do so. You are of course not yet dying except in a peculiar, philosophically long-sighted sense but have for long been storing memories, since death's waiting room may not be far off.

Which brings the thought of how awful it would be if we could learn in advance, even well in advance, the likely date of our death. Some sufferers from cancer are told this, though prescription there is happily not yet an exact science. One is sometimes told of sufferers who receive such news stoically, with courage if not equanimity; and sometimes with that. Perhaps it has become a medico-social custom to report such responses, but not the horrified reactions.

Bad as that is, it would be little better to be told by a superior being that, though you are at present in very good health, you are ordained to die on an exact date some years hence. That would give time for a range of responses, from: 'Well, it's a good way off', to long and increasing fear as the clock remorselessly ticks. Worse would be if the manner of your death were indicated so that, from then on you feared to board an aeroplane or walk under a ladder or indulge in certain foods, your equivalent of a surfeit of lampreys. You know you are doomed to die on, by or under, one of them, though at the actual moment you will probably be taken by surprise.

Apparently St Charles Borromaeus remarked that, if suddenly called to die, he would continue his game of chess; a game played not only for pleasure but to honour God.

Naturally, there are more regretful than composed utterances about the condition not only of becoming old, but also of entering a period of almost waiting for death; not counting the days but being aware that they might well be counted if only one knew how. And meanwhile, experience, perhaps, a first startling act of neglect, or of casually being set aside, physically or socially, by a few younger people.

I first met that in my mid-seventies, waiting to board a tube train. There was a crowd. Just ahead of me an elderly lady, foot already on the step, was being roughly pushed aside by a coarse-looking man of about 40. 'Do let that lady get on,' I said to him. 'Shut yer fucking trap, yer old sod,' he said, and went on pushing. Not a significant incident; it could have happened to someone in their forties. For me, the strange indicative thing was that I was surprised even then to be called 'old', not at being sworn at.

Another instance showed what I suppose might be called unconscious ageism (though it is sad to think of any intelligent person displaying ageism and yet not being aware of it), occurred quite recently. I was asked to introduce a broadcast discussion on the justification for the BBC licence fee; not a fashionable arrangement to defend. To my surprise, I was introduced by the presenter as one 'who was born ten

years before the BBC was founded'. To what in the subject
or the later discussion was the date of my birth likely to be
relevant? Was it meant to suggest that I could take a long,
considered view? Or was it a way of discounting in
advance, on the ground of age, anything that the old sod
might say? Was it, as I was inclined to think from its tone,
an instance of 'youthism', which is much promoted today
and, incidentally, does its bit to wear away the sense of the
meaningfully connected three-tier family. As do some other
shifts of fashion and outlook.

That odd preliminary sentence also explained a quizzical
and dubious expression I had seen in that presenter's eye
during an advance discussion we had had about the
subject. It was silently registering: 'Not one of our generation, a real oldie, out-of-touch, with nothing of interest or
relevance to say nowadays'. But not as extreme as one of
ageism's more brutal appellations: 'A waste of space'.

I may have been too much affected by these 'ignore the
old' attitudes. Having been brought up by my grandmother
from 8 to 18 (for her, from seventy-odd to eighty-odd), I
have long felt a special link with old women and old men.
As I have already said, the sight of one crying out from grief
or despair or pain is one of the most deeply disturbing
experiences I know. I once saw an old man whose hand had
just been trapped in a forcefully shut car door. His cries
were heart-rending, not easily to be forgotten. That anyone
so old should suffer so much!

Shakespeare writes movingly of: 'Unregarded age in
corners thrown' (*As you Like It*); which by curious contrast
calls up today's common style towards the old – not
thrown into a corner but put carefully into one of those,
we all hope, 'very nice' Old People's Homes and visited as
often as possible.

It is, all too naturally, to be expected that comments on
the unpleasantness of old age should outnumber those on

its pleasures. Among the oddest is one by a man who at that point had certainly not reached old age, but who insisted that he felt like it. In one of his letters to Clough, Matthew Arnold regretted that at past 30 he felt three-parts iced over. Typical, that, of him. But we know what he meant, what he felt like. It would be silly to think one had the right to poke fun. He probably felt tired, overworked, overstressed, short of money, plagued by 'sick fatigue' and 'languid doubt'; and Oxford's splendid time of youth very far back.

That is typical of aspects of old age for very many who feel truly old, if not at thirty-odd then at sixty-odd. There can be then a lack of hope and expectation, a sense of 'just seeing things out', or of them seeing you out, of plodding on as though used up, subject to odd but continuous aches and pains which do not kill but can depress. Few if any recurrent thoughts that there is 'always tomorrow', new things to look forward to, new busy-nesses. It is hard to be gracefully resigned to the recurring indications of age's progress.

Here is a simple but common contrast. When young, we look forward to a long life; but not to becoming old. When we are indeed old we look back and think young people careless, wasteful of the gifts of their time.

In the circumstances it can be surprising that so many in their seventies and even eighties can seem so sprightly, especially old men doing the family shopping in the local supermarket, smiling at the check-out assistants through their NHS specs and full set of NHS dentures, members of the 'It's being so cheerful that keeps me going' club.

Henry James, as he fell from his first stroke, which could well have been fatal, heard 'a voice': 'So here it is at last, the distinguished thing.' That has a kind of nobility.

Ways of Facing

Roughly speaking there are, as to attitudes towards life when death nears, three kinds of old people. First, the depressed and unhopeful; then the putters-up with things, who are 'just managing', 'can't grumble' and who recognize every day that 'Things could be worse.' Then, at the far end, are the more resilient, who accept old age and live through it happily each day, until they 'pop their clogs'. On the whole, only the brave or the not very imaginative can live like that; and even they would need to be free from crippling pain.

As we saw much earlier, Tennyson was one of the great acceptors: 'But every hour is saved / From that eternal silence, something more…'; and: 'Old age hath yet his honour and his toil; / Death closes all'; and yet again: 'Tho' much is taken, much abides.' All those are from the magnificent *Ulysses*. Tennyson is one of the great romantics about death. Sometimes he seems almost to relish such thoughts. Reading him, one is occasionally tempted to respond: 'Speak for yourself. Death can't come too late for me.' Yet the movement of such lines can almost persuade us to accept their haunting burden, or at least to suspend judgement on what they are saying. Tennyson's *In Memoriam* is more convincing.

Wordsworth accepted and so did Spenser. Browning, working through dramatic characters, could express both acceptance and depression; on balance, the acceptance seems to dominate for him.

In many writers the main expectation is of an unwelcome or even shocking obliteration. Above all, silence is feared, an eternal silence, as though the failure to make contact, to connect, through speech or touch or glance, will be the worst to be borne of all Death's characteristics. Inevitably.

Shakespeare, as so often and in so much, captures best the fear; and, above all the sheer physical horror which visits some, as in *Measure for Measure*: 'Aye, but to die and go we know not where / To lie in cold obstruction and to rot.' Of all such passages I know, and of all such thoughts, that is the most elemental, claustrophobic to the highest and endless degree.

After the depressed and the 'just managing' types – to refer back to that three-part classification – are those who have found a sort of contentment in their later days, and seem to accept the idea of death with equanimity; or who *manage* rather than just 'putting up' with things. They are happier than their 'can't grumble' companions in the middle group. They keep going along, not unhappily.

Easier to accept, I used to think and often quote, would be (at not too great an age) Edgar's harsh wisdom, in *King Lear*: 'Men must endure / their going hence, even as their coming hither: / Ripeness is all.' After seeing Parkinson's and Alzheimer's at work I have begun to find that less bracing. How brave and grand those words seem, but by now how far from any such strength many of us might find ourselves retaining.

We sometimes feel, especially if we are very old indeed, like surprised left-overs, in shrinking time and fading light. We are at that last departure point, watching as the convoy just before us, and its suitably geriatric music, fades into the dark. Or, to change the image, this is Death's Reception Area where the magazines, like us, are tattered and out of date, no longer relevant, slightly irritating and importunate reminders to a few of those watching from the shore. Get on with it.

And what of suicide? How does one come round to self-destruction? By many routes, presumably. It is plain that some sad solo agents are more fragile than others, always near the edge; others seem too robust ever to near it – that point where life seems simply no longer worth living. Pain, constant severe pain, can also lead to that full stop. For some, memories have stopped bringing any consolation, nothing to feed on, and the present has become insupportable. The scaffolding of the personality has fallen away; the sense of the self seems no longer worth sustaining; a considered judgement is made.

I wonder whether the most moving kind of suicide was chosen by a friend, who seemed quite unable to bear life after his wife died. If so, even an agnostic can hope for some consolation for them on the other side: a blinding light and then – 'Here I am, love'; and a joyous 'And about time, too.'

At this point there comes to mind Thoreau's astonishing, blank and sometimes inescapable assertion in *Walden*: 'The mass of men lead lives of quiet desperation.' That nags, so I return to it constantly. 'Many' men do; but 'the mass'? The powerful hold of the claim comes from that 'quiet'. If it had run: 'Most men live lives of desperation' one could more easily take it or leave it; it wouldn't so greatly hold. Even less would apply to: 'Most men lead desperate lives'; that could be argued about in the clear, to and fro, calmly, not trapped by the basilisk effect of that 'quiet'; and 'desperate lives' is more down-to-earth than 'lives of desperation'. 'Of quiet desperation' haunts because the desperation is quietly and permanently ('so long as life is lived') suffered. Endured.

John Webster's summing-up, in *The White Devil*, about the nature of life as it edges inexorably towards death – ''Tis better to be fortunate than wise' – grips for its dour suggestiveness. It may, we have to admit, be true. More's the pity. The lucky fool is not a favourite figure; he hasn't had to work for his good fortune. We wish it were otherwise.

Short of suicide, thoughts on the nearness of death can produce formidably contradictory aphorisms; especially on the last day, or the endless day. The first enjoins us to 'live this day as if thy last'; another exhorts us always to act as though we will live forever. The first tells us to seize the day, cram it with the best experiences we already know or with others new to us, because none may follow. There may be no tomorrow. Do nothing of which you would feel ashamed. Leave a pleasant smell behind you.

The other main injunction is more difficult to paraphrase. Obviously it means first that we should not fear or be absorbed by the thought of death since that attitude will freeze our will, cause us to give remaining things – emotional experiences, events – their full due, their flavour and meaningfulness. It may make us sloppily casual and unwilling, no more open to being 'surprised by joy', ready to face fully what might be the still arresting and fulfilling 'thisness' of things. Neither skimp nor gobble; neither rush nor ignore.

Depending on mood, I seem to swing between the two epigrams, though leaning more toward the second. As so often, E. M. Forster put this memorably, when he recommended that we behave as if we are immortal and society eternal ('What I Believe'). Characteristically, he added that, though these beliefs may be mistaken, they will help us to keep open a few breathing holes for the human spirit. Yes.

Those Gone Before

Nowadays, when I pick up the morning's newspapers, I look first at the obituaries; then back to Page 1 for the day's news.

So, another daily thought is of those who have gone – or just gone – before. Here, Shakespeare was almost unbearably poignant, on the: 'Precious friends hid in death's dateless night' (*Sonnets*, 30), and elsewhere.

Among Thoughts of Death

By now, the dead are many and of all kinds; relatives, close friends, acquaintances and some we never met but took as models, good or bad. The thoughts are made worse because so many were younger than ourselves. Some were treasured 'ironic points of light' (Auden, 'September 1, 1939'), and some no better than they should have been, but 'whose works / Were in better taste than their lives' (Auden, 'At the Grave of Henry James').

Siblings, of course, and about the two of mine I have written at length elsewhere. Brother Tom died of cancer; he had been a model to Molly and me. Molly died only recently, worn out. Gillian, one of her four daughters, said that almost her last words were: 'I want to be buried near me mum.' She had been only 6 when our mother died so her memory must have been very shadowy; but she had clung to the idea of her mother for almost 80 years. What for us turned the screw at that near-final moment was a fact she had forgotten: a search two years before had led to the conclusion that our mother had been buried in an unmarked paupers' grave. I think Gillian decided to scatter her ashes somewhere near that unhappy piece of land.

The oddest surprise of all is that you, an agnostic, still have a slight but ineradicable feeling that those who have 'gone before', especially those from whom you tried to learn, are still watching, sometimes shaking their heads.

You suddenly remember someone of your own age who was once close but with whom you have not been in touch for many years; and the thought emerges: 'He must be dead by now.' You don't quite believe that, since you are yourself still down here. So then you think that he may well be somewhere still reachable, perhaps having similar occasional thoughts about you. Up in Leeds for one night after many years, I looked in the Telephone Directory. He was there, only about a dozen miles away up on the edge of Wharfedale. I phoned. 'Oh, Richard, I *am* sorry. He died last year,' said his widow, and I felt for a long moment a sense of dereliction. That gap should not have been allowed to occur.

Earlier, I mentioned three types who bear old age in different ways. There are, it is now obvious, some who face death very calmly; and there are those who can hardly bear the thought. The second people, I suspect, are in a majority; more fear than accept or welcome. Those who bear with courage the thought of both extreme age and death have their spokesmen and women. Such was the robust Alice James; in a letter to William she wrote: 'It is so comic to hear oneself called old, even at 90, I suppose.' That stiffens our sinews, especially if the casual dress of retirement has occasionally become, and indicates, a form of final carelessness. That last noun seems to occur in these pages more often than I would have expected.

There are those who imagine they can play final games with their God, or Fate; the 'between the stirrup and the ground' gamblers, one of whom appears in Graham Greene's *Brighton Rock*, who bet on making amends at the last minute, and then being able to slip under the gate just before it closes. A Roman Catholic offering.

Among many of his judgements on death, Bacon called it: 'The least of all evils'. At least one modern writer joined him there, as brave and direct – Stevie Smith, with: 'If there wasn't death, I think you couldn't go on.' A kinship across the centuries there, between the assured and the less assured – 'I think' – but grimmer. And again a kind of embracing death like a bride, at least by one of them.

Some find a certain kind of comfort in the conviction that all life is eternally present, in old age and in death; all our yesterdays remain. Into the most extreme old age? And after death? Some, perhaps many, do believe so. Again: 'not lost, but gone before'. Our attitudes to death are at least as complex in old age as those we had, if any, when young;

sometimes similar, sometimes opposites. In youth we hardly believe in death. In old age we sometimes say or act as if we believed: 'Death, where is thy sting'; but not: 'Death, thou shalt die' – which belongs to another realm of belief. The mind can practise an endless urge to comfort itself at each stage; but not in everyone. On the other front, which perhaps includes many of us, there is no firmly assumed afterwards.

A Brief Change of Perspective

As to the down-to-earth, to society now. We can acknowledge some clear gains, at least in our fortunate and at bottom self-absorbed part of the world. Those gains are obvious, so most do not need listing. Let us say simply 'better health and longer life' (so long as that last is felt to be a boon), more care for the poor (but not enough), better education (but badly divided in its provision). Within Britain, class divisions are somewhat fainter, chiefly by being partly overlaid with the two-dimensional panorama of emerging meritocracy and that at different levels.

What of the long-term future? Hope survives as it always does but needs to be heavily qualified. Neighbourliness survives and so does much charitable activity. At weekends, especially in the cities, brutality flourishes.

Much of the above seems slight in comparison with other considerations. We are now able to annihilate ourselves; humanity, that is – whether by weapons of mass destruction or, more slowly, by raping the environment. Sometimes one feels like a small object walking precariously and for the time being on the surface of a huge and doomed ball.

Are some married people now deciding not to have children, because they cannot confidently envisage a future for them? That seems likely, of a few. But most will go on going on, as is our wont; just assuming – if we think of the matter – that somehow things will sort themselves out.

Closing

Here we need to approach the deepest perspective of all.

Tennyson's greatly moving rhetorical poem, *Ulysses*, comes to mind yet again after all these pages; about facing death:

> I am a part of all that I have met;
> ...
>
>   you and I are old;
> Old age hath yet his honour and his toil;
> Death closes all: but something ere the end,
> Some work of noble note may yet be done.

With that, one feels like recovering the old-fashioned word 'dauntless'. We need all we can find of such baggage.

Thoreau, we may recall, said that it is as hard to see into the self as to see the back of one's own neck. True, but there are mirrors which can help to assess the good and bad in us all, even if held by ourselves; and which will support, or not, what others have directly seen. As with certain kinds of writing; a little, but something.

In old age I have come to recognize that anger, even on behalf of good causes, no longer becomes you; this being too easily tempted to become hot under the collar. If you can manage it, irony, mickey-taking, wryness, are better, especially in these times and at this age. And still too the willingness, in the admirable American expression, to 'hang on in there'.

A sort of basic cheerfulness remains, not so prompt now, but still there. Sometimes, I do not know why, a kind of intermittent gloominess or unexpectancy intervenes and escapes into the writing. I was delighted when one of our sons, noticing an omission in a description of our family life, said: 'You forgot to say we laughed a lot.' It is of course easier, almost mandatory, in this kind of writing to display one's weaknesses and not one's virtues; if those can be safely found.

Compensations? Much the greatest is that of always having someone near to talk to intimately. Not to gossip; but to exchange anecdotes, yes. To talk about all personal things, and to try to make better sense of the world around you, by being as open and honest as you can manage. Couples who use their intimacy to shore up their satisfaction with themselves and each other, and so to belittling others, are easily recognizable. Still – let there be charity, as early as possible, to them as to others.

I have quoted a lot throughout, perhaps too much. But two final quotations are needed. First, the magnificently resisting end of Kafka's *The Trial*. K refuses the proposal by the anonymous officials, 'the partners', that he should kill himself rather than being killed by them. No. *They* have to do it, not he [they do so, with a knife and K utters his last words]. '"Like a dog!", he said: it was as if he meant the shame of it to outlive him.' He makes his judgement on death at the very end; it is a shameful thing, the process, the event; it is as meaningless as a dog's death. But because K can see that and '*find words*' for it, an image, he can judge it. And in a certain sense surmount but not escape it.

As so often, Shakespeare captures in one sentence, by a superb image (which I love to recall wherever possible), revulsion before death and a courageous putting-up with – or defying – it. Berowne in *Love's Labour's Lost* is ordered, before being allowed to press his proposal of marriage, to work for a year in hospitals, where most are

143

faced with an early and perhaps extremely painful end. He must learn, in an awe-inspiring yet uplifting prescription: 'To move wild laughter in the throat of death.' In spite of all that dread, this suggests a madly brave energy: not to give in, not to be pitied, to recognize that you've had a good run – and, if not, that your spirit can share with others the ability to express courage; and laugh – even to the end.

Yeats has that fine passage quoted much earlier, from 'Sailing to Byzantium', exhorting the soul to clap its hands and sing in old age: 'for every tatter in its mortal dress'. That, yes, going on going on, almost certainly tattered; but with, one hopes, the right mixture of adjutant attitudes – above all, love and charity.

That seems as good a way as any to sign off here.